DIABETIC MICROWAVE COOKBOOK

■ ■ ■ ■ ■ ■ ■

Mary Jane Finsand

Foreword by
James D. Healy,
M.D., F.A.A.P.

Sterling Publishing Co., Inc.   New York

Edited by Laurel Ornitz

Recipe Consultant: Carol Tiffany

Library of Congress Cataloging-in-Publication Data

Finsand, Mary Jane.
    Diabetic microwave cookbook / Mary Jane Finsand; foreword by
James D. Healy.
        p.   cm.
    ISBN 0-8069-6957-1. —ISBN 0-8069-6960-1 (pbk.)
    1. Diabetes—Diet therapy—Recipes. 2. Microwave cookery.
    I. Title.
RC662.F5664   1989   89-19693
641.5′6314—dc20   CIP

Copyright © 1989 by Mary Jane Finsand
Published by Sterling Publishing Co., Inc.
387 Park Avenue South, New York, N.Y. 10016
Distributed in Canada by Sterling Publishing
% Canadian Manda Group, P.O. Box 920, Station U
Toronto, Ontario, Canada M8Z 5P9
Distributed in Great Britain and Europe by Cassell PLC
Artillery House, Artillery Row, London SW1P 1RT, England
Distributed in Australia by Capricorn Ltd.
P.O. Box 665, Lane Cove, NSW 2066
Manufactured in the United States of America

Contents

Foreword

Although the *Diabetic Microwave Cookbook* was written specifically for the diabetic, it is an excellent overall kitchen reference for preparing a variety of foods in a minimum of time. Many people on normal diets have difficulty planning and preparing meals with sufficient contrasts. Creating diversity in an already restricted diet can be even more challenging; however, users of Mary Jane Finsand's diabetic cookbooks know that they can prepare and eat hundreds of delicious dishes and still follow a doctor-prescribed diet.

Mary Jane has included many new and exciting recipes in this book that are easy to prepare and delicious to eat. Each recipe is complete with calorie and food-exchange information to allow users to regulate food intake within their diet.

The *Diabetic Microwave Cookbook* undoubtedly will be one of your most frequently used cookbooks. Share it with your friends and family —I am confident that they will confirm my high recommendation.

James D. Healy, M.D., F.A.A.P.

A Note from Covenant Medical Center

Here's a wonderful new cookbook for diabetics with the built-in bonus of speed. Mary Jane Finsand's new *Diabetic Microwave Cookbook* allows you to stay on your diet without the hassle of time-consuming meal preparation. Now, for the first time, there is a diabetic cookbook jammed full of fabulous recipes that take only minutes to prepare. With this added convenience, you'll have more time to spend on making your meals more fun, nutritious, and creative. We know that you will find the *Diabetic Microwave Cookbook* to be a valuable resource in meal planning.

Hattie M. Middleton, R.D.
Darlene K. Duke, R.N.

Convenant Medical Center
Waterloo, Iowa

Introduction

The speed of the microwave oven allows you to create delicious, nourishing dishes that would normally be too time-consuming to prepare. I developed the recipes in the *Diabetic Microwave Cookbook* with three factors in mind: easy preparation, good taste, and convenience. In addition, I selected ingredients that you can find in any supermarket.

I have placed a major emphasis on meat dishes because in discussing diets, and diets for diabetics in particular, I have found that many people do not have time to prepare meat and meat dishes from scratch because they take so long to cook. Of course, I have also included various side dishes—such as potatoes, rice, pasta, vegetables, and many of your other favorite foods.

To get the most from the *Diabetic Microwave Cookbook,* you might want to use it differently from other cookbooks. Instead of selecting individual recipes to try, you might set aside a week or two and devote that time to microwave cooking. This way, you'll be able to experience firsthand how using the microwave can enhance your cooking—and how easily you can maintain your proper diet with it.

I dedicate this book to modern people of all ages who want to feel their very best by following their individual diets—whether diabetic or otherwise. I hope you get as much out of this book as I've tried to put in it.

Mary Jane Finsand

You & Your Microwave

Microwave ovens come in different sizes and with different power levels. Like any skill, microwaving takes a little practice. Until you become completely familiar with your particular microwave—with its speed and energy levels—you may over- or undercook.

The recipes in this book have been developed for microwaves of standard size and power levels. HIGH is full power (100 percent) and is used for food that can cook at a fast heat. MEDIUM is about 50 percent power and is used for foods that would require much more attention if cooked on HIGH. MEDIUM HIGH is about 70 percent power; if your microwave unit cooks too fast on HIGH or too slow on MEDIUM for some of the recipes, you might want to try the MEDIUM HIGH level. LOW is about 30 percent power and is used for delicate foods or slow simmering. WARM is about 10 percent power and will keep foods that are already cooked hot.

Microwaving Tips

It is very easy to overcook in a microwave. Of course, turning the dish and rearranging food are more important when you are using microwaves that do not contain a food rotator. Rearranging food allows all of the food in the dish to cook evenly. Always stir food from the outside of the dish towards the middle when microwaving. The food closer to the outside will cook faster, just as the food on the bottom of a pan on a normal range will cook faster. Resting time is also very important in microwaving since cooking continues after you have taken the food out. You might want to undercook at first, allowing the food to finish cooking during the resting period.

Containers for Microwaving

The most common microwave dish is either plastic or glass. There are many dishes made just for microwave cooking. These are the best to use because the microwaves can pass through them and cook the food. When you are cooking for a short period of time, these dishes will remain cool. But if you prolong the cooking time, the dish will become hot from the transference of the heat from the hot food. It's always wise to use hot pads when removing *any* container from the microwave.

Paper plates and cups as well as other paper products can be used in the microwave; however, be careful because prolonged cooking can cause paper to burn. Sometimes you may want to use aluminum foil to slow down the cooking of a certain part of a food, such as the tips of a chicken. Foil trays of ¾ in. (18 cm) or less can be used in most microwaves.

Covering Microwave Containers

Porous covers, such as paper napkins and paper towels, allow steam to escape. Any time you do not want the food to become moist or want to thicken a sauce, it is best to use paper. Semiporous covers, such as wax paper, hold in heat for faster cooking while allowing most of the steam to escape. Tight covers, such as plastic wrap and glass or plastic lids, hold in steam as well as heat. Tight covers should be used on any food that requires moisture and heat to tenderize or cook it throughly. *Always be very careful when removing a tight cover—steam burns can be very painful.*

Using the Recipes—Conversion Guides, Flavorings & Extracts, Spices & Herbs

Read the recipes carefully; then assemble all equipment and ingredients. Use standard measuring equipment (whether metric or customary), and be sure to measure accurately. Remember, these recipes are good for everyone, not just the diabetic.

Customary Terms

t.	teaspoon	qt.	quart
T.	tablespoon	oz.	ounce
c.	cup	lb.	pound
pkg.	package	°F	degrees Fahrenheit
pt.	pint	in.	inch

Metric Symbols

mL	millilitre	°C	degrees Celsius
L	litre	mm	millimetre
g	gram	cm	centimetre
kg	kilogram		

Conversion Guide for Cooking Pans and Casseroles

Customary	Metric
1 qt.	1 L
2 qt.	2 L
3 qt.	3 L

Oven-Cooking Guides

Fahrenheit °F	Oven Heat	Celsius °C
250–275°	very slow	120–135°
300–325°	slow	150–165°
350–375°	moderate	175–190°
400–425°	hot	200–220°
450–475°	very hot	230–245°
475–500°	hottest	250–290°

Use this candy thermometer guide to test for doneness:

Fahrenheit °F	Test		Celsius °C
230–234°	Syrup:	Thread	100–112°
234–240°	Fondant/Fudge:	Soft Ball	112–115°
244–248°	Caramels:	Firm Ball	118–120°
250–266°	Marshmallows:	Hard Ball	121–130°
270–290°	Taffy:	Soft Crack	132–143°
300–310°	Brittle:	Hard Crack	149–154°

Guide to Approximate Equivalents

Customary				Metric	
Ounces Pounds	Cups	Tablespoons	Teaspoons	Millitres	Grams Kilograms
			¼ t.	1 mL	1 g.
			½ t.	2 mL	
			1 t.	5 mL	
			2 t.	10 mL	
½ oz.		1 T.	3 t.	15 mL	15 g.
1 oz.		2 T.	6 t.	30 mL	30 g.
2 oz.	¼ c.	4 T.	12 t.	60 mL	
4 oz.	½ c.	8 T.	24 t.	125 mL	
8 oz.	1 c.	16 T.	48 t.	250 ml	
2.2 lb.					1 kg.

Keep in mind that this guide does not show exact conversions, but it can be used in a general way for food measurement.

Guide to Baking-Pan Sizes

Customary	Metric	Holds	Holds (Metric)
8-in. pie	20-cm pie	2 c.	600 mL
9-in. pie	23-cm pie	1 qt.	1 L
10-in. pie	25-cm pie	1¼ qt.	1.3 L
8-in. round	20-cm round	1 qt.	1 L
9-in. round	23-cm round	1½ qt.	1.5 L
8-in. square	20-cm square	2 qt.	2 L
9-in. square	23-cm square	2½ qt.	2.5 L
9 × 5 × 2 loaf	23 × 13 × 5 cm (loaf)	2 qt.	2 L
9-in. tube	23-cm tube	3 qt.	3 L
10-in. tube	25-cm tube	3 qt.	3 L
10-in. Bundt	25 cm Bundt	3 qt.	3 L
9 × 5 in.	23 × 13 cm	1½ qt.	1.5 L
10 × 6 in.	25 × 16 cm	3½ qt.	3.5 L
11 × 7 in.	27 × 17 cm	3½ qt.	3.5 L
13 × 9 × 2 in.	33 × 23 × 5 cm	3½ qt.	3.5 L
14 × 10 in.	36 × 25 cm	cookie tin	
15½ × 10½ × 1 in.	39 × 25 × 3 cm	jelly roll	

Flavorings & Extracts

Orange, lime, and lemon peels give vegetables, pastries, and puddings a fresh, clean flavor. Liquor flavors, such as brandy and rum, give cakes and other desserts a company flair. Choose from the following to give your recipes some zip, without adding calories:

Almond	Butter Rum	Pecan
Anise (Licorice)	Cherry	Peppermint
Apricot	Chocolate	Pineapple
Banana Creme	Coconut	Raspberry
Blackberry	Grape	Rum
Black Walnut	Hazelnut	Sassafras
Blueberry	Lemon	Sherry
Brandy	Lime	Strawberry
Butter	Mint	Vanilla
Butternut	Orange	Walnut

Spices & Herbs

These are some of my favorite spices and herbs. They will definitely add distinction to your dishes, without adding calories.

Allspice: Cinnamon, ginger, nutmeg flavor; used in breads, pastries, jellies, jams, pickles.

Anise: Licorice flavor; used in candies, breads, fruit, wine, liqueurs.

Cinnamon: Pungent, sweet flavor; used in pastries, breads, pickles, wine, beer, liqueurs.

Clove: Pungent, sweet flavor; used for ham, sauces, pastries, puddings, fruit, wine, liqueurs.

Coriander: Butter-lemon flavor; used for cookies, cakes, pies, puddings, fruit, wine and liqueur punches.

Ginger: Strong, pungent flavor; used in anything sweet, plus with beer, brandy, liqueurs.

Nutmeg: Sweet, nutty flavor; used in pastries, puddings, vegetables.

Woodruff: Sweet vanilla flavor; used in wines, punches.

Appetizers

Stuffed Mushrooms

20 large	white mushrooms	20
⅓ c.	diced onion	90 mL
2 T.	cornflake crumbs	30 mL
2 T.	fine bread crumbs	30 mL
2 T.	grated Parmesan cheese	30 mL
3 T.	dry sherry	45 mL
	water	
	parsley flakes	
	salt and pepper	
	garlic powder (optional)	

Wash and clean the mushrooms; then pull off the stems and dice. Place the diced stems and onions in a small bowl, and cover with wax paper. With the microwave on HIGH, cook for 45 seconds. Add the crumbs, cheese, sherry, and enough water to moisten the mixture. Season to taste with parsley flakes, salt, pepper, and garlic powder. Then spoon the filling into the mushroom caps. Place them around the edge of a large round microwave plate. Cook on MEDIUM for 3 minutes, turning the plate every minute for even cooking. Serve hot.

Yield: 20 servings
Exchange, 1 serving: negligible
Calories, 1 serving: 12
Carbohydrates, 1 serving: 3

Greek-Style Mushrooms

1 lb.	button mushrooms	500 g
1 c.	water	250 mL
½ c.	olive oil	125 mL
2 T.	lemon juice	30 mL
2 cloves	garlic, minced	2 cloves
1 T.	celery seed	15 mL
1 T.	white vinegar	15 mL
1	bay leaf, crushed	1
1 t.	salt	5 mL
¼ t.	fennel seed	1 mL
¼ t.	oregano	1 mL
¼ t.	whole black pepper, slightly crushed	1 mL

Clean the mushrooms and remove just the soiled end of the stem. Set aside. Combine the remaining ingredients (not the mushrooms) in a 2 qt. (2 L) microwave casserole or bowl. With the microwave on HIGH, cook for 5 to 6 minutes. Remove from the microwave, and cover with a lid or plastic wrap. Allow to rest for 5 minutes. Stir in the mushrooms. Return to the microwave, uncovered, and cook on MEDIUM for 3 minutes. Stir every 60 seconds. Chill at least 24 hours before serving. To serve: Remove the mushrooms with a slotted spoon and place them on a bed of parsley or endive.

Yield: 20 servings
Exchange, 1 serving: negligible
Calories, 1 serving: negligible
Carbohydrates, 1 serving: negligible

Steamed Oysters

12	oysters in shells	12
1 T.	low-calorie margarine	15 mL
½ t.	fresh lemon juice	2 mL
dash	Tabasco sauce	dash

Scrub and rinse the oysters under cold running water. Place the oysters around the edge of a large microwave plate (two may go in the middle if necessary.) With the microwave on HIGH, cook for 5 to 7 minutes or until the shells open; turn the plate every 3 minutes for even cooking. Remove the oysters from their shells with a shucking knife. Place them on heated dish and keep them warm. Meanwhile, combine the margarine, lemon juice, and Tabasco sauce in a small microwave dish. Cook on HIGH 20 to 25 seconds or until the margarine is melted. Serve with the oysters.

Yield: 4 servings
Exchange, 1 serving: ½ medium-fat meat
Calories, 1 serving: 45
Carbohydrates, 1 serving: negligible

Crab Dip

8 oz.	cream cheese	240 g
6 oz.	crabmeat, frozen or canned	170 mL
2 T.	skim milk	30 mL
1 T.	sherry wine	15 mL
2 t.	grated fresh lemon rind	10 mL
1 t.	grated horseradish	5 mL

Combine the ingredients in a 1½ qt. (1½ L) bowl. With the microwave on MEDIUM, cook 6 to 8 minutes, rotating one-quarter turn every minute until done.

Yield: 16 servings
Exchange, 1 serving (dip only): 1 fat
Calories, 1 serving (dip only): 51
Carbohydrates, 1 serving (dip only): negligible

Tavern Dip

8 oz.	cream cheese	240 g
10 oz.	Old English cheese spread	300 g
⅓ c.	dark beer	90 mL
1½ t.	Worcestershire sauce	7 mL
2 T.	imitation bacon bits	30 mL

Combine the ingredients in a 1½ qt. (1½ L) bowl. With the microwave on MEDIUM, cook 6 to 8 minutes, rotating one-quarter turn every minute until the mixture is done.

Yield: 16 servings
Exchange, 1 serving (dip only): 2 fat
Calories, 1 serving (dip only): 92
Carbohydrates, 1 serving (dip only): negligible

Hot Bean Dip

17 oz. can	refried beans	451 g can
½ c.	red salsa sauce	125 mL
⅓ c.	reduced-calorie sour cream	90 mL
2 T.	dried onion flakes	30 mL
⅛ t.	cayenne pepper	½ mL
⅓ c.	shredded sharp Cheddar cheese	90 mL

Combine refried beans, salsa sauce, sour cream, and dried onion flakes in a 1½ or 2 qt. (1½ or 2 L) microwave bowl. With the microwave on MEDIUM, cook for 5 to 7 minutes, stirring the mixture and turning the bowl every 2 minutes. Next, stir in cayenne pepper and sprinkle with shredded cheese. Return to the microwave and cook on MEDIUM 1 to 2 minutes longer or until the cheese is melted and hot.

Yield: 16 servings
Exchange, 1 serving (spread only): ½ bread
Calories, 1 serving (spread only): 33
Carbohydrates, 1 serving (spread only): 5

Crab on Crackers

7 oz. can	crabmeat	210 g can
2 T.	cornstarch	10 mL
¼ t.	marjoram	1 mL
dash	garlic salt	dash
¼ c.	finely chopped celery	60 mL
3 T.	finely chopped onion	45 mL
¼ c.	reduced-calorie mayonnaise	60 mL
36	round crackers	36

Drain the liquid from the crabmeat into a small microwave bowl or measuring cup. Stir in the cornstarch until dissolved. Stir in the marjoram and garlic salt. With the microwave on HIGH, cook for 30 seconds. Stir and return to the microwave for 30 more seconds if the mixture is not clear and thickened. Allow to cool. Flake the crabmeat. Combine the flaked crabmeat, celery, onion, and mayonnaise in a bowl. Stir in the crab liquid. Divide the crabmeat mixture evenly between the 36 crackers. Place 12 crackers in a circle around the edge of a paper plate (do the same for two more plates). With the microwave on HIGH, cook for 30 seconds; then rotate the plate one-half turn and continue cooking for 15 seconds more.

Yield: 18 servings
Exchange, 1 serving: ½ bread; ¼ medium-fat meat
Calories, 1 serving: 59
Carbohydrates, 1 serving: 6

Clam Dip

8 oz.	cream cheese	240 g
½ c.	minced clams	125 mL
1 T.	clam juice	15 mL
1 t.	Worcestershire sauce	5 mL
1 t.	lemon juice	5 mL
¼ t.	salt	1 mL

Combine the ingredients in a 1½ qt. (1½ L) bowl. With the microwave on MEDIUM, cook 6 to 8 minutes, rotating one-quarter turn every minute until done.

Yield: 16 servings
Exchange, 1 serving (dip only): 1 fat
Calories, 1 serving (dip only): 50
Carbohydrates, 1 serving (dip only): negligible

Shrimp Dip

8 oz.	cream cheese	240 g
6 oz.	shrimp, frozen or canned	170 g
2 t.	horseradish mustard	10 mL
2 t.	ketchup	10 mL
1 t.	dried onion flakes	5 mL
¼ t.	garlic salt	2 mL

Combine the ingredients in a 1½ qt. (1½ L) bowl. With the microwave on MEDIUM, cook for 6 to 8 minutes, rotating one-quarter turn every minute until done.

Yield: 16 servings
Exchange, 1 serving (dip only): 1 fat
Calories, 1 serving (dip only): 57
Carbohydrates, 1 serving (dip only): negligible

Nachos

⅓ c.	nacho cheese soup	90 mL
2 T.	water	30 mL
1 t.	Worcestershire sauce	5 mL
1 qt.	large corn chips	1 L
2 T.	chopped pimiento	30 mL

Combine the cheese soup, water, and Worcestershire sauce in a micro-wave bowl or measuring cup. Stir to blend. Cover lightly with wax paper. With the microwave on HIGH, cook for 1 minute, stirring after 30 seconds. Place the chips in a shallow microwave platter. Pour the cheese mixture over the top. Cook in the microwave, uncovered, for 30 seconds, stirring or folding to rearrange the chips. Return to the micro-wave for 30 to 40 seconds. Top with the chopped pimiento just before serving.

Yield: 36 servings
Exchange, 1 serving: 1 bread; 2 fat
Calories, 1 serving: 166
Carbohydrates, 1 serving: 16

Appetizer Wieners

4	beef wieners	4
¼ c.	ketchup	60 mL
3 T.	water	45 mL
1 T.	mustard	15 mL
1 t.	Worcestershire sauce	5 mL
¼ t.	onion powder	1 mL

Cut the wieners into eighths and place them on a microwave plate or paper plate. Combine the remaining ingredients in a small bowl. Brush half of the mixture over the wieners. With the microwave on HIGH, cook for 1½ minutes, rotating the plate one-half turn after 1 minute. Brush with the remaining sauce mixture. Continue cooking on HIGH for 1 minute. Place a toothpick in the top of each wiener piece.

Yield: 16 servings
Exchange, 1 serving: ⅓ high-fat meat
Calories, 1 serving: 43
Carbohydrates, 1 serving: negligible

Bite-Size Pepperoni Pizza

4	English muffins	4
8 oz. jar	pizza sauce	240 g jar
½ c.	finely chopped onions	125 mL
8 rings	green pepper, quartered	8 rings
16 slices	pepperoni, cut in half	16 slices
1 c.	shredded mozzarella cheese (reduced-calorie)	250 mL

Split the muffins in half and toast them in the toaster. Spread the pizza sauce on both halves of the muffins. Top with the onions. Cut each muffin half into four pieces. Place the eight muffin pieces in a circle around the edge of a paper plate (four plates will be used). Lay one-quarter section of the green pepper on top of each muffin piece. Place one-half slice of the pepperoni on top of each muffin piece. Top evenly with the mozzarella cheese. Place each plate, uncovered, in the microwave, and cook on HIGH for 1 minute; rotate each plate one-half turn after 30 seconds.

Yield: 32 servings
Exchange, 1 serving: ¼ bread; ⅓ medium-fat meat
Calories, 1 serving: 45
Carbohydrates, 1 serving: 3

Asparagus Wrap

10	asparagus spears	10
2 T.	Dijon mustard	30 mL
1 T.	reduced calorie mayonnaise	15 mL
10 large slices	bologna	10 large slices

Trim the bottom end of the asparagus and blanch with boiling water. Blend the mustard and mayonnaise in a small bowl. Divide and spread the mustard mixture evenly on the large bologna slices. Wrap one asparagus spear in each bologna slice. Place the slices in a single layer on a round microwave platter or plate. Cover lightly with paper towels. With the microwave on MEDIUM, cook for 1 minute or until hot; rotate the plate one-half turn after 30 seconds.

Yield: 10 servings
Exchange, 1 serving: 1 high-fat meat
Calories, 1 serving: 86
Carbohydrates, 1 serving: 2

Soups & Beverages

Beef-Vegetable Soup

2 lbs.	utility or chunk beef	1 kg
1 large	soup bone	1 large
1½ qt.	water	1½ L
4	peppercorns	4
2	whole cloves	2
2	bay leaves	2
2 T.	finely chopped onion	30 mL
2 T.	finely grated carrot	30 mL
1 T.	finely chopped celery leaves	15 mL
1 T.	finely chopped fresh parsley	15 mL
1 t.	salt	5 mL
1 t.	sweet marjoram	5 mL
1 t.	sweet basil	5 mL
2 c.	diced potatoes	500 mL
3	tomatoes, diced	3
1 c.	coarsely chopped onion	250 mL
1 c.	snap green beans	250 mL
1 c.	sliced celery	250 mL
¾ c.	diced carrots	190 mL
	salt and pepper to taste	

Trim the meat of any excess fat; then cut it into small pieces. Place the meat and soup bone in a 4 qt. (4 L) microwave casserole or soup pot. Cover with a lid or plastic wrap. With the microwave on HIGH, cook for 4 minutes, stirring after 2 minutes. Add the water, peppercorns, cloves, bay leaves, 2 T (30 mL) finely chopped onion, 2 T. (30 mL) finely chopped carrot, celery leaves, parsley, 1 t. (5 mL) salt, sweet marjoram, and sweet basil. Re-cover and continue cooking on HIGH for 15 minutes or until the mixture begins to boil. Stir, reduce heat to MEDIUM, and cook for 45 minutes or until the meat is fork-tender. Remove the soup bone; then remove any meat from the bone, and return the meat to the soup. Add the remaining vegetables. Season to taste with salt and pepper. Re-cover and cook with the microwave on MEDIUM for 12 to 15 minutes or until the vegetables are tender.

Yield: 12 servings
Exchange, 1 serving: 1 high-fat meat, ½ vegetable
Calories, 1 serving: 167
Carbohydrates, 1 serving: 4

Country Barley Soup

2 t.	vegetable oil	10 mL
½ c.	medium barley	125 mL
1 stalk	celery, thinly sliced	1 stalk
1	onion, minced	1
1 T.	all-purpose flour	15 mL
6 c.	cold water	1500 mL
⅓ t.	instant vegetable broth mix	90 mL
¼ c.	dry milk powder	60 mL

Pour the vegetable oil into a 8 in. (20 cm) glass or microwave pie pan. Turn the pan to cover the bottom with oil—heating slightly in the microwave, if necessary. Add the barley, celery, and onion. Cover with plastic wrap. Cook in the microwave for 2 minutes. Combine the flour, cold water, and vegetable broth in a large casserole. Stir to dissolve the flour. Add the barley mixture. With the microwave on HIGH, cook for 10 minutes or just to boiling. Stir and continue cooking on MEDIUM LOW for 15 minutes more or until the barley is tender. Stir in the dry milk powder. Allow to rest for 5 minutes before serving.

Yield: 6 servings
Exchange, 1 serving: 1½ bread
Calories, 1 serving: 126
Carbohydrates, 1 serving: 20

Lentil Soup

5 c.	water	1250 mL
2 c.	dried lentils	500 mL
1 lb	lean ground beef	500 g
3 cans (16 oz. each)	tomatoes	3 cans (484 g each)
½ c.	chopped onions	125 mL
2	bay leaves	2
1 t.	chili powder	5 mL
½ t.	thyme	2 mL
	salt and pepper to taste	

Combine the water and lentils in a 4 qt. (4 L) microwave casserole or soup pot; then cover with a lid or plastic wrap. With the microwave on HIGH, cook for 20 minutes. Crumble and stir the meat into the hot lentils. Stir in the remaining ingredients. Cover and cook on MEDIUM for 20 to 25 minutes, sirring occasionally. Allow the soup to rest for 5 minutes before serving. Add salt and pepper to taste.

Yield: 10 servings
Exchange, 1 serving: 1 bread, 1 medium-fat meat, 1 vegetable
Calories, 1 serving: 188
Carbohydrates, 1 serving: 21

Spicy Tomato Bouillon

2 c.	chopped tomatoes	500 mL
1 c.	water	250 mL
2 t.	instant beef broth mix	10 mL
¼ t.	celery seeds	1 mL
¼ t.	peppercorns	1 mL
3	whole cloves	3
	salt to taste	

Combine the ingredients in 2 qt. (2 L) bowl or measuring cup. Cover lightly with plastic wrap. Cook on MEDIUM for 4 minutes or until just boiling. Strain before serving.

Yield: 4 servings
Exchange, 1 serving: 1 vegetable
Calories, 1 serving: 23
Carbohydrates, 1 serving: 4

Cabbage Soup

16 oz. can	tomatoes	484 g can
2 c.	shredded cabbage	500 mL
1 c.	canned beef broth	250 mL
¼ c.	chopped onion	60 mL
1	bay leaf, crushed	1
	salt and pepper to taste	

Pour the liquid of the tomatoes into a 3 qt. (3 L) casserole or bowl. Chop the tomatoes and add them to the liquid. Add the remaining ingredients. Cover with a lid or plastic wrap. Cook on HIGH for 4 minutes; then stir and continue cooking on MEDIUM for 12 to 15 minutes or until the cabbage is tender. Divide evenly into four bowls.

Yield: 4 servings
Exchange, 1 serving: 1½ vegetable
Calories, 1 serving: 40
Carbohydrates, 1 serving: 9 g

Cabbage and Beet Soup

1 small head	cabbage, shredded	1 small head
16 oz. can	diced beets with liquid	485 g can
1	onion, diced	1
2 qts.	water	2 L
5 T.	instant beef broth mix	75 mL
8 slices	sourdough bread	8 slices

Combine the cabbage, beets with liquid, and onion in a 4 qt. (4 L) microwave casserole or soup pot. Cover with a lid or plastic wrap. With the microwave on HIGH, cook for 5 to 6 minutes or until the cabbage is crisp-tender. Add the water and broth mix. Stir to thoroughly mix. Recover and continue cooking on HIGH for 6 minutes or until the mixture just comes to a boil. Stir. Place a piece of sourdough bread in a flat soup bowl; then ladle the soup over the bread.

Yield: 8 servings
Exchange, 1 serving: 1 bread, 1 vegetable
Calories, 1 serving: 103
Carbohydrates, 1 serving: 6

Cream of Chicken Soup

1 c.	skim milk	250 mL
1 c.	low-fat cottage cheese	250 mL
1 c.	diced cooked chicken	250 mL
3 c.	water	750 mL
3 T.	instant chicken broth mix	45 mL
3 T.	finely chopped onion	45 mL

Combine the milk and cottage cheese in a food processor or blender. Mix to a smooth consistency. Pour into a 2 qt. (2 L) bowl or measuring cup. Add the remaining ingredients. With the microwave on MEDIUM, cook for 2 minutes. Stir and reduce the temperature to LOW; then continue cooking on LOW for 5 minutes or until the soup is hot.

Yield: 4 servings
Exchange, 1 serving: 1 lean meat, ⅔ low-fat milk
Calories, 1 serving: 121
Carbohydrates, 1 serving: 9

Chicken-Shrimp Gumbo

2 c.	water	500 mL
2 T.	instant chicken broth mix	30 mL
16 oz. can	whole tomatoes	484 g can
1 c.	sliced celery	250 mL
½ c.	chopped onion	125 mL
2	bay leaves	2
½ t.	thyme	2 mL
3 T.	all-purpose flour	45 mL
4 oz.	boneless chicken breast	120 g
½ lb.	uncooked shrimp, peeled and deveined	250 g
2 c.	hot cooked rice	500 mL
If desired:		
½ c.	sliced mushrooms	125 mL
2	peppercorns	2

Combine the water, chicken broth mix, and liquid from the tomatoes in a 3 qt. (3 L) casserole. Cook, uncovered, with the microwave on HIGH for 2 minutes. Stir to disolve the broth mix. Cut or chop the tomatoes. Add the tomatoes, celery, onion, bay leaves, and thyme to the liquid. Slowly stir in the flour. If desired, add the mushrooms and peppercorns. Cook, uncovered, with the microwave on HIGH for 6 minutes. Reduce the heat to MEDIUM LOW, stir, and cook for 2 minutes longer. Remove the skin for the chicken breast and cut the breast into large cubes or pieces. Add to the gumbo mixture. With the microwave on MEDIUM, cook for 6 minutes. Cover and allow to rest for 5 minutes or until the chicken is tender. Add the shrimp; then return to the microwave and cook on MEDIUM for 4 minutes longer or until the shrimp is pink and thoroughly cooked. To serve: Place ¼ c. (125 mL) of the hot cooked rice in the bottom of a large soup bowl. Ladle one eighth of the gumbo on top.

Yield: 8 servings
Exchange, 1 serving: ⅔ bread, 1 lean meat, 1 vegetable
Calories, 1 serving: 151
Carbohydrates, 1 serving: 17

Quick Borscht

16 oz. can	whole baby beets	484 g can
10 oz. can	condensed beef consommé	265 g can
½ c.	water	125 mL
1	bay leaf	1
1 T.	lemon juice	15 mL
1 T.	granulated sugar replacement	15 mL
2	eggs	2
2 T.	water	30 mL

Combine the liquid from the baby beets, the beef consommé, the ½ c. (125 mL) water, and bay leaf in a 3 qt. (3 L) casserole or bowl. With the microwave on HIGH, cook for 4 minutes. Shred two thirds of the beets; slice the remaining one third of the beets. Add the beets to the liquid. With the microwave on MEDIUM, cook for 2 minutes or until the liquid is boiling. Stir in the lemon juice and sugar replacement. Beat the two eggs with the 2 T. (30 mL) of water. Slowly pour the egg mixture into the soup mixture, stirring constantly so that the eggs will not curdle. Serve hot.

Yield: 4 servings
Exchange, 1 serving: ½ high-fat meat, 1 vegetable
Calories, 1 serving: 83
Carbohydrates, 1 serving: 5

Fresh Garden Soup

1	carrot, diced	1
1 small	turnip, diced	1 small
½ c.	shredded cabbage	125 mL
1 T.	reduced-calorie margarine	15 mL
3 c.	water	750 mL
2 T.	instant beef broth mix	30 mL
2	green onions, sliced	2
½ c.	fresh green peas	125 mL
1 small	potato, diced	1 small
	salt and pepper to taste	

Sauté the carrot, turnip, and cabbage in the margarine in a microwave skillet or pie pan on HIGH for 3 to 5 minutes. Stir occasionally. Transfer to a 2 qt. (2 L) microwave casserole or baking dish. Add the water, broth mix, green onions, peas, and potato. Add salt and pepper to taste. Cover with a lid or plastic wrap. With the microwave on MEDIUM, cook for 15 to 20 minutes or until the vegetables are tender.

Yield: 4 servings
Exchange, 1 serving: ½ bread
Calories, 1 serving: 7
Carbohydrates, 1 serving: 7

Potato Soup

1 c.	chopped onions	250 mL
1 c.	thinly sliced celery	250 mL
⅓ c.	grated carrot	90 mL
2½ c.	diced potatoes	625 mL
2 T.	water	30 mL
1½ T.	all-purpose flour	21 mL
1 qt.	skim milk	1 L
	salt and pepper to taste	
	finely chopped parsley	

Grease a 3 qt. (3 L) dish with vegetable-oil spray. Add the onions, celery, carrots, potatoes, and water. Cover with a lid or plastic wrap. With the microwave on HIGH, cook for 4 or 5 minutes or until the potatoes are tender. Sprinkle the flour over the vegetables and stir. Slowly pour the milk over the mixture. Stir to completely blend. Season to taste with salt and pepper. Cover and cook on HIGH in the microwave for 3 minutes, stirring and turning the dish one-half rotation. Continue cooking on HIGH for 8 minutes or until the soup is thickened, turning the dish once. Garnish with parsley.

Yield: 8 servings
Exchange, 1 serving: ½ bread, ½ skim milk, ½ vegetable
Calories, 1 serving: 98
Carbohydrates, 1 serving: 9

Split Pea Soup

2 c.	dried split peas (yellow or green)	500 mL
5 c.	hot water	1250 mL
2	onions, chopped	2
1	carrot, shredded	1
2	bay leaves	2
⅓ c.	sliced celery	90 mL
2 t.	parsley	10 mL
dash	cayenne pepper	dash
	salt to taste	

Place the peas in a large mixing bowl; then cover with hot water and allow to soak overnight. Drain the peas and place them in a 4 qt. (4 L) microwave casserole or soup pot. Add the 5 c. (1250 mL) water. With the microwave on HIGH, cook for 40 minutes. Stir in the remaining ingredients. Cover with a lid or plastic wrap. With the microwave on MEDIUM, cook for 20 to 25 minutes. If desired, puree the soup in a blender.

Yield: 8 servings
Exchange, 1 serving: 1 bread
Calories, 1 serving: 88
Carbohydrates, 1 serving: 16

French Onion Soup

4	onions, thinly sliced	4
1 T.	reduced-calorie margarine	15 mL
1 qt.	water	1 L
3 T.	instant beef broth mix	45 mL
½ t.	Worcestershire sauce	2 mL
	pepper	
4 slices	thin French bread, toasted	4 slices
2 T.	grated Parmesan cheese	30 mL

Combine the onion and margarine in a microwave skillet or pie pan. With the microwave on HIGH, cook for 6 to 7 minutes. Stir occasionally. Transfer to a 2 qt. (2 L) microwave casserole or baking dish. Add the water, broth mix, Worcestershire sauce, and pepper to taste. Cover with a lid or plastic wrap. With the microwave on HIGH, cook for 6 to 8 minutes or until the mixture is very hot. Place the French bread slices in four soup bowls; then ladle the soup over the bread. Evenly sprinkle the Parmesan cheese over the top.

Yield: 4 servings
Exchange, 1 serving: 1 bread, 1 vegetable
Calories, 1 serving: 110
Carbohydrates, 1 serving: 21

Carrot Soup

1 T.	reduced-calorie margarine	15 mL
1	onion, sliced	1
1 T.	all-purpose flour	15 mL
1 qt.	water	1 L
3	beef or chicken bouillon cubes	3
3 c.	sliced carrots	750 mL
1½ c.	thinly sliced celery with leaves	375 mL
	pepper to taste	

Combine the margarine and sliced onions in a 3 qt. (3 L) microwave casserole or baking dish. With the microwave on HIGH, cook for 3 to 4 minutes or until the onions are limp. Blend in the flour. Add the water and bouillon cubes. Return to the microwave and continue cooking on HIGH for 6 minutes or until boiling. Add the remaining ingredients. Cover with a lid or plastic wrap. With the microwave on HIGH, cook for

3 minutes. Test the vegetables for doneness; then, if necessary, return the soup to the microwave and cook on MEDIUM for 2 more minutes.

Yield: 8 servings
Exchange, 1 serving: 1 vegetable
Calories, 1 serving: 24
Carbohydrates, 1 serving: 4

Mixed Fruit Drink

1 c.	orange juice	250 mL
1 c.	unsweetened grapefruit juice	250 mL
1 c.	unsweetened pineapple juice	250 mL
½ t.	nutmeg	2 mL
½ t.	cardamom	2 mL

Combine all the ingredients in a 2 qt. (2 L) casserole or bowl. Cook, uncovered, in the microwave on HIGH for 7 minutes or until the mixture is hot.

Yield: 6 servings
Exchange, 1 serving: 1 fruit
Calories, 1 serving: 59
Carbohydrates, 1 serving: 14

Spiced Pineapple Beverage

2 c.	unsweetened pineapple juice	500 mL
6 whole	cloves	6 whole
½ t.	cinnamon	2 mL
¼ t.	nutmeg	1 mL

Combine all the ingredients in a 1 qt. (1 L) microwave casserole or bowl. Cook, uncovered, in the microwave for 6 to 7 minutes or just until boiling.

Yield: 4 servings
Exchange, 1 serving: 1 fruit
Calories, 1 serving: 70
Carbohydrates, 1 serving: 17

Tangy Grape-Grapefruit Beverage

2	lemons, thinly sliced	2
2 c.	water	500 mL
⅔ c.	granulated sugar replacement	180 mL
2 c.	grape juice	500 mL
2 c.	pink grapefruit juice	500 mL

Combine the lemon slices and water in a 3 qt. (3 L) microwave casserole or bowl, and cover with a lid or plastic wrap. With the microwave on MEDIUM, cook for 10 minutes. Stir in the remaining ingredients. Cook, uncovered, on MEDIUM 5 to 6 minutes more or until boiling. If desired, remove the lemon slices before serving.

Yield: 4 servings
Exchange, 1 serving: 2 fruit
Calories, 1 serving: 130
Carbohydrates, 1 serving: 36

Spiced Hot Chocolate

¼ c.	cocoa	60 mL
1½ T.	granulated fructose	21 mL
3 c.	skim milk	750 mL
2 t.	grated orange rind	10 mL
½ t.	nutmeg	2 mL
¼ t.	cinnamon	1 mL
	cinnamon sticks (optional)	

Combine the cocoa and fructose in a 2 qt. (2 L) casserole or microwave bowl. Stir in enough milk to make a pastelike mixture, about ½ c. (125 mL). Stir in the remaining milk. Cover with a lid or plastic wrap. With the microwave on HIGH, cook for 3 to 4 minutes or until warm. Stir in the orange rind, nutmeg, and cinnamon. Return to the microwave, uncovered, and cook on MEDIUM for 4 to 5 minutes or until the chocolate is hot. If desired, place a cinnamon stick in each mug before pouring in the chocolate.

Yield: 3 servings
Exchange, 1 serving: 1 skim milk, ⅓ fruit
Calories, 1 serving: 97
Carbohydrates, 1 serving: 18

Quickbread &
Sandwiches

Microwaving Muffins

# Muffins	Cooking Time
1	30 seconds to 1 minute
2	1 to 2 minutes
3	1½ to 2½ minutes
4	2 to 3 minutes
5	2 ½ to 3 ½ minutes
6	3 to 5 minutes

Basic Muffins

2 c.	all-purpose flour	500 mL
4 t.	baking powder	20 mL
½ t.	salt	2 mL
¼ c.	granulated sugar replacement	60 mL
1	egg, beaten	1
¼ c.	vegetable oil	60 mL
1 c.	skim milk	250 mL

Sift the dry ingredients together. Combine the egg, vegetable oil, and skim milk in a bowl; then beat with a fork to blend. Pour the liquid mixture into the dry mixture. Stir just enough to moisten the flour. Fill microwave containers half full. With the microwave on MEDIUM HIGH, cook for the length of time given in the chart above. The muffins are done when a toothpick inserted in the middle comes out clean.

Yield: 14 servings
Exchange, 1 serving: 1 bread
Calories, 1 serving: 93
Carbohydrates, 1 serving: 13

Bran Muffins

1 c.	all-purpose flour	250 mL
1 c.	whole bran cereal	250 mL
¼ c.	granulated sugar replacement	60 mL
1 T.	baking powder	15 mL
½ t.	salt	2 mL
1	egg, beaten	1
¾ c.	skim milk	190 mL
¼ c.	vegetable oil	60 mL

Combine the dry ingredients in a large mixing bowl. Beat the egg, skim milk, and oil together until well blended. Pour into the dry mixture. Stir just enough to moisten the flour and bran cereal. Fill microwave containers half full. With the microwave on MEDIUM HIGH, cook for the length of time given in the chart on page 31. The muffins are done when a toothpick inserted in the middle comes out clean.

Yield: 14 servings
Exchange, 1 serving: 1 bread
Calories, 1 serving: 90
Carbohydrates, 1 serving: 12

Yellow Cornmeal Muffins

1 c.	all-purpose flour	250 mL
1 c.	yellow cornmeal	250 mL
4 t.	baking powder	20 mL
1 t.	salt	5 mL
⅓ c.	granulated sugar replacement	90 mL
1	egg, beaten	1
¼ c.	vegetable oil	60 mL
1 c.	skim milk	250 mL

Combine the dry ingredients in a large mixing bowl. Combine the egg, vegetable oil, and skim milk in a bowl; then beat with a fork to blend. Pour the liquid mixture into the dry mixture, stirring just enough to moisten the flour. Fill microwave containers half full. With the microwave on MEDIUM HIGH, cook for the length of time given in the chart on page 31. The muffins are done when a toothpick inserted in the middle comes out clean.

Yield: 14 servings
Exchange, 1 serving: 1 bread
Calories, 1 serving: 89
Carbohydrates, 1 serving: 15

Pineapple Coffee Cake

2 c.	all-purpose flour	500 mL
2 t.	baking powder	10 mL
5 T.	granulated sugar replacement	75 mL
½ t.	salt	2 mL
⅓ c.	reduced-calorie margarine	90 mL
1	egg, beaten	1
⅓ c.	skim milk	90 mL
1½ c.	diced pineapple in its own juice, drained	375 mL
¼ c.	granulated brown sugar replacement	60 mL
3 T.	reduced-calorie margarine	45 mL
3 T.	all-purpose flour	45 mL

Sift the flour, baking powder, 5 T. (75 mL) sugar replacement, and salt together. Cut in the margarine. Combine the egg and milk. Mix slightly, pour into the flour mixture, and blend thoroughly. Spread the batter into two greased 9 in. (23 cm) round microwave baking dishes. Evenly arrange the diced pineapple on top of the batter. Combine the ¼ c. (60 mL) brown sugar replacement and the remaining ingredients. Sprinkle evenly over both dishes. Cook individually, uncovered, on MEDIUM HIGH for 7 to 8 minutes or until a toothpick inserted in the middle comes out clean. Rotate the dish one-quarter turn after 2 minutes— then every 2 minutes until a toothpick inserted in the middle comes out clean. (If you are using a rack, cook both dishes at the same time on MEDIUM HIGH for 9 to 10 minutes. Rotate as above and change the position of the pans after 4 minutes.) Remove the coffee cake from the microwave, cover it with wax paper, and allow it to rest 8 to 10 minutes before serving.

Yield: 16 servings
Exchange, 1 serving: ⅔ bread
Calories, 1 serving: 67
Carbohydrates, 1 serving: 9

"Mix" Coffee Cake

2 c.	biscuit mix	500 mL
1	egg, slightly beaten	1
⅔ c.	water	180 mL
1 T.	granulated sugar replacement	15 mL

Combine the ingredients in a mixing bowl. Blend thoroughly. Transfer to a greased 9 in. (23 cm) round microwave baking dish. Cook, uncovered, on MEDIUM HIGH in the microwave for 5 to 6 minutes or until a toothpick inserted in the middle comes out clean; rotate the dish one-half turn every 2 minutes or use a food rotator. Cover with wax paper and allow to rest 7 to 10 minutes before serving.

Yield: 8 servings
Exchange, 1 serving: 1⅓ bread
Calories, 1 serving: 105
Carbohydrates, 1 serving: 18

Almond Biscuit Ring

¼ c.	granulated brown sugar replacement	60 mL
2 T.	dietetic maple syrup	30 mL
2 T.	reduced-calorie margarine	30 mL
2 t.	water	10 mL
⅓ c.	coarsely chopped almonds	90 mL
8 oz. tube	refrigerator biscuits	240 g tube

Combine the brown sugar replacement, maple syrup, margarine, and water in a 1½ qt. microwave casserole or 8 in. (20 cm) round baking dish. With the microwave on HIGH, cook for 1 minute. Cover with a paper towel and allow the margarine to completely melt. Stir in the almonds. Cut the biscuits into fourths and roll them into small balls. Add these biscuit balls to the syrup mixture, tossing to coat each ball. Arrange the balls around the outside edge of the casserole. Place the casserole on the food rotator. With the microwave on MEDIUM, cook for 5 to 6 minutes. Remove from the microwave, cover with wax paper for 4 minutes, and then turn out onto a serving plate.

Yield: 10 servings
Exchange, 1 serving: 1 bread
Calories, 1 serving: 81
Carbohydrates, 1 serving: 15

Canadian Bacon Cheese Sandwich

1 T.	chopped onion	15 mL
1 T.	chopped mushroom	15 mL
1 T.	chopped celery	15 mL
1 T.	chopped green pepper	15 mL
1	bun (hamburger style)	1
2	thin slices of Canadian bacon	2
2 (½ oz. each)	thin slices of Swiss cheese	2 (15 g each)

Combine the onion, mushroom, celery, and green pepper in a small microwave custard cup or measuring cup. With the microwave on HIGH, cook for 30 seconds. Slice the bun in half. Place the bottom of the bun on a paper towel–lined plate. Top with the Canadian bacon, cheese, and onion mixture. With the microwave on HIGH, cook for 2 to 2½ minutes or until the cheese is slightly melted. Place the top of the bun in the microwave, and continue cooking on HIGH for 20 seconds. Place the top of the bun over the sandwich mixture.

Yield: 1 serving
Exchange, 1 serving: 1 bread, 1⅓ high-fat meat
Calories, 1 serving: 208
Carbohydrates, 1 serving: 16

Salmon Sandwiches

8 oz. can	salmon	240 g can
¼ c.	reduced-calorie mayonnaise	60 mL
1 T.	horseradish	15 mL
½ t.	lemon juice	2 mL
10 slices	rye bread	10 slices

First, drain, debone, and flake the salmon. Then add the mayonnaise, horseradish, and lemon juice to the salmon, stirring to mix thoroughly. Spread evenly on five slices of bread. Place on a paper towel–lined plate. With the microwave on HIGH, cook for 2 minutes. Top with the remaining slices of bread, and continue cooking on HIGH for 30 seconds.

Yield: 5 servings
Exchange, 1 serving: 2 bread, 1 lean meat
Calories, 1 serving: 227
Carbohydrates, 1 serving: 28

Potatoes

Boiled Potatoes

½ c.	water	125 mL
½ t.	salt	125 mL
2 c.	potato chunks	500 mL

Combine all the ingredients in a microwave bowl, and cover tightly with plastic wrap. With the microwave on HIGH, cook for 5 minutes. Carefully remove the plastic wrap, and stir the potatoes to rearrange them. Return to the microwave and continue cooking on HIGH for 4 to 5 minutes. With the water remaining in the bowl, either drain or whip.

Yield: 3 servings
Exchange, 1 serving: 1 bread
Calories, 1 serving: 81
Carbohydrates, 1 serving: 15

Parmesan Potatoes

2 c.	hot Boiled Potatoes, mashed (see above)	500 mL
¼ c.	grated Parmesan cheese	60 mL
	freshly chopped parsley	

Stir the Parmesan cheese into the hot potatoes. Cover lightly with wax paper. With the microwave on MEDIUM, cook for 2 minutes, stirring once. Transfer to a serving bowl. Sprinkle with chopped parsley.

Yield: 3 servings
Exchange, 1 serving: 1 bread, ⅓ high-fat meat
Calories, 1 serving: 118
Carbohydrates, 1 serving: 16

French Potato Salad

2 c.	hot Boiled Potatoes, drained (page 36)	500 mL
1	hard-cooked egg, sliced	1
½ c.	reduced-calorie mayonnaise	125 mL
¼ c.	sliced celery	60 mL
2 T.	chopped onion	30 mL
1 T.	mustard	15 mL
2 t.	celery seed	10 mL
	salt and pepper to taste	

Combine all the ingredients in a bowl. Stir to mix completely. Cover and refrigerate until chilled.

Yield: 4 servings
Exchange, 1 serving: 1 bread
Calories, 1 serving: 85
Carbohydrates, 1 serving: 16

Potato with Basil Sauce

2 c.	hot Boiled Potatoes, drained (page 36)	500 mL
2 T.	reduced-calorie margarine	30 mL
2 t.	dark basil	10 mL
1 clove	garlic, sliced	1 clove
½ t.	thyme	2 mL

Have the potatoes prepared for the recipe. Melt the margarine in a shallow microwave platter or plate. Stir in the basil, garlic, and thyme. With the microwave on HIGH, cook for 30 seconds. Add the potatoes; then fold to completely coat them. Return to the microwave, uncovered, and cook on HIGH for 2 to 3 minutes, stirring or folding every 60 seconds.

Yield: 4 servings
Exchange, 1 serving: 1 bread
Calories, 1 serving: 79
Carbohydrates, 1 serving: 15

Buttermilk Potatoes

2 medium	potatoes	2 medium
1/4 c.	buttermilk	60 mL
2 T.	reduced-calorie margarine	30 mL
8 oz. can	mushroom stems and pieces, drained	224 g can
1 T.	onion flakes	15 mL
1/4 t.	ground thyme	1 mL

Wash the potatoes, cutting out any dark spots. Wrap the wet potatoes in plastic wrap. With the microwave on HIGH, cook for 5 minutes or until the potatoes are soft. Remove the plastic wrap from the potatoes, and then peel the potatoes under cold running water. Rice or mash the potatoes into a medium-size bowl. Add the remaining ingredients and stir to mix. If needed, cover with plastic wrap and reheat for several minutes on MEDIUM HIGH in the microwave.

Yield: 2 servings
Exchange, 1 serving: 1 bread, 1 fat
Calories, 1 serving: 130
Carbohydrates, 1 serving: 16

Easy Sweet Potatoes

23 oz. can	sweet potatoes	651 g can
1/2 c.	undiluted frozen orange juice concentrate	125 mL
1/2 t.	cinnamon	2 mL
1/4 t.	nutmeg	1 mL
1/4 t.	ginger	1 mL

Drain the sweet potatoes, reserving 1/2 c. (125 mL) of liquid. Combine the sweet potatoes, reserved sweet potato liquid, and remaining ingredients in a medium-size bowl. Mash thoroughly. Cover with wax paper; then cook on MEDIUM in the microwave for 6 to 7 minutes or until the potatoes are hot.

Yield: 8 servings
Exchange, 1 serving: 1 1/3 bread
Calories, 1 serving: 90
Carbohydrates, 1 serving: 20

Sweet, Creamy Mashed Potatoes

1 env.	nondairy whipped topping mix	1 env.
(to make 2 c.)		(to make 500 mL)
½ c.	skim milk	125 mL
1 qt.	hot mashed potatoes	1 L
	paprika	

Combine the whipped topping and skim milk in a mixing bowl. Beat to whip. Place half of the mashed potatoes in a greased 2 qt. (2 L) microwave casserole or baking dish. Top with half of the whipped topping. Repeat layers. With the microwave on MEDIUM, cook for 3 to 4 minutes. Sprinkle with paprika.

Yield: 8 servings
Exchange, 1 serving: 1⅓ bread
Calories, 1 serving: 120
Carbohydrates, 1 serving: 19

Potatoes with Chives

2 large	potatoes	2 large
⅓ c.	skim milk	90 mL
1 T.	reduced-calorie salad dressing	15 mL
½ c.	chopped chives	125 mL
	salt and pepper	

Wash the potatoes, cutting out any dark spots. Wrap the wet potatoes in plastic wrap. With the microwave on HIGH, cook for 5 minutes or until the potatoes are soft. Remove the plastic wrap from the potatoes and peel the potatoes under cold running water. Mash the potatoes into a medium-size bowl. Add the remaining ingredients, sirring to mix. If needed, cover with plastic wrap and reheat for several minutes on MEDIUM HIGH in the microwave.

Yield: 4 servings
Exchange, 1 serving: 1 bread
Calories, 1 serving: 96
Carbohydrates, 1 serving: 17

Potatoes with Sour Cream

4 medium	potatoes, cubed	4 medium
½ c.	water	125 mL
⅓ c.	minced onion	90 mL
½ t.	salt	2 mL
⅛ t.	black pepper	½ mL
¼ c.	imitation sour cream	60 mL
3 T.	finely chopped parsley	45 mL
	paprika	

Combine the potatoes, water, onion, and salt in a microwave bowl. Cover with plastic wrap. With the microwave on HIGH cook for 6 to 7 minutes or until tender; stir once during cooking. Do not drain. Fold in the black pepper and sour cream. Transfer to a serving dish. Sprinkle with parsley and paprika.

Yield: 4 servings
Exchange, 1 serving: 1 bread, 1 fat
Calories, 1 serving: 138
Carbohydrates, 1 serving: 16

German Potato Salad

4 large	potatoes	4 large
½ c.	water	125 mL
¼ c.	white vinegar	60 mL
1 T.	all-purpose flour	15 mL
1	onion, chopped	1
2 slices	crisp cooked bacon	2 slices
¼ t.	salt	1 mL
⅛ t.	black pepper	½ mL
	freshly chopped parsley	

Wash the potatoes, cutting out any dark spots. Wrap the wet potatoes in plastic wrap. With the microwave on HIGH, cook for 5 to 7 minutes or until the potatoes are soft. Rearrange the potatoes after 2 minutes. Carefully remove the plastic wrap from the potatoes and peel the potatoes under cold running water. Slice the potatoes into a large bowl. Meanwhile, combine the water, vinegar, and flour in a microwave bowl. Stir to blend and dissolve the flour. Then stir in the chopped onion. With the microwave on HIGH, cook for 3 to 4 minutes—stirring after 1 minute, then every 30 seconds. Crumble the bacon. Stir in the bacon, salt, and pepper. Return to the microwave and cook on MEDIUM for 2 to 3 minutes or until the mixture is thickened. Pour the mixture over the hot potatoes. Fold slightly to coat the potatoes. Garnish with freshly chopped parsley.

Yield: 8 servings
Exchange, 1 serving: 1 bread
Calories, 1 serving: 77
Carbohydrates, 1 serving: 14

Stuffed Potatoes

1 large	baking potato	1 large
1 T.	skim milk	1 mL
2 t.	reduced-calorie margarine	10 mL
	salt and pepper	
2 t.	shredded sharp Cheddar cheese	10 mL

Wash the potato and then prick it in several places with a fork. Wrap the potato in plastic wrap. With the microwave on HIGH, cook the potato for 5 to 6 minutes or until it feels soft. Cut the potato in half lengthwise and scoop out the insides. Set aside the two potato skins. Mash the potato with skim milk and margarine. Add salt and pepper to taste. Then place the mashed potato back into the skins. Sprinkle with Cheddar cheese. Place the two potato halves on a microwave plate. With the microwave on MEDIUM, cook for 1½ to 2 minutes or until the cheese is melted.

Yield: 2 servings
Exchange, 1 serving: 1 bread, 1 fat
Calories, 1 serving: 125
Carbohydrates, 1 serving: 15

Pasta

Plain Pasta

1 qt.	water	1 L
	salt, if desired	
8 oz.	pasta*	

*Noodles, macaroni, shells, lasagna, spaghetti, vermicelli, linguine, or any other type of pasta.

For smaller or broken pasta, use a 2 or 3 qt. (2 or 3 L) casserole with a lid or cover with plastic wrap.

For long thin pasta, such as spaghetti or vermicelli, use either a 9 × 13 in. (13 × 33 cm) dish or a 2 or 3 qt. glass measuring cup and cover with plastic wrap.

For long, wide pasta, such as lasagna, use a 9 by 13 in. (23 × 33 cm) microwave or glass dish and cover with plastic wrap.

Combine the water and salt in a dish (the salt is optional). Cover and cook with the microwave on HIGH for 8 to 10 minutes or until the water is boiling. Add the pasta, stirring to allow the water to circulate around each pasta piece. Cover and cook with the microwave on MEDIUM for 6 to 10 minutes, stirring occasionally to prevent sticking.

Yield: 12 servings
Exchange, 1 serving: 1 bread
Calories, 1 serving: 75
Carbohydrates, 1 serving: 15

Shells in Cream Sauce

2 c.	water	500 mL
2 c.	medium-sized shell noodles	500 mL
	salt	

½ c.	thinly sliced carrots	125 mL
⅓ c.	chopped celery	90 mL
¼ c.	chopped onion	60 mL
1 T.	low-calorie margarine	15 mL
¾ c.	skim milk	190 mL
4 t.	all-purpose flour	20 mL
	salt and pepper to taste	

Pour the water into a 2 qt. (2 L) casserole with a cover. Add the shell noodles and some salt as desired; then stir. Cover and cook with the microwave on HIGH for 7 minutes. Add the carrots, celery, and onion; then stir to mix. Cover and cook with the microwave on HIGH for 5 minutes. Stir the margarine into the mixture. Combine the milk and flour in a shaker or cup, blending thoroughly. Pour and stir it into the noodle mixture. Cover and cook with the microwave on HIGH for 2 minutes. Stir and allow to set for 3 to 4 minutes before serving. Add salt and pepper to taste.

Yield: 12 servings
Exchange, 1 serving: 1 bread
Calories, 1 serving: 82
Carbohydrates, 1 serving: 16

Rotini and Peas Italiano

2 c.	water	500 mL
1¾ c.	rotini macaroni	440 mL
1 c.	frozen green peas	250 mL
1 T.	salad dressing	15 mL
1 T.	low-calorie Italian dressing	15 mL

Combine the water and rotini in a 2 qt. (2 L) casserole. Stir and cover. With the microwave on HIGH, cook for 5 minutes. Stir and cook on MEDIUM for 5 minutes. Stir in the peas. With the microwave still on MEDIUM, cook for 2 minutes. Drain thoroughly. Return the mixture to the casserole dish. Add the salad dressing and Italian dressing; then stir to completely blend. With the microwave still on MEDIUM, cook for 2 minutes.

Yield: 12 servings
Exchange, 1 serving: 1 bread
Calories, 1 serving: 86
Carbohydrates, 1 serving: 16

Clam Chowder and Ham Bake

1½ c.	spaghetti, broken into 1 in. (2.5 cm) pieces	375 mL
2 c.	water	500 mL
1 T.	salad oil	15 mL
2 c.	chopped broccoli	500 mL
19 oz. can	New England clam chowder	539 g can
½ c.	cubed turkey ham	125 mL
3 T.	water	45 mL

Spray a 3 qt. (3 L) microwave dish and cover with vegetable-oil spray. Add the broken spaghetti, water, and salad oil. Stir to moisten all the spaghetti. With the microwave on HIGH, cook, covered, for 7 minutes. Add the broccoli; then stir and cook on MEDIUM for 4 minutes. Drain thoroughly. Return the noodles and broccoli to the microwave dish. Stir in the remaining ingredients. Return to the microwave and cook on HIGH for 4 minutes.

Yield: 12 servings
Exchange, 1 serving: 1 bread, ¼ lean meat
Calories, 1 serving: 91
Carbohydrates, 1 serving: 16

Spaghetti Francisco

2 c.	spaghetti, broken into 1 in. (2.5 cm) pieces	500 mL
2 c.	water	500 mL
1 T.	salad oil	15 mL
2 slices	bacon, diced	2 slices
1 small	onion, chopped	1 small
½	green pepper, chopped	½
8 oz. can	tomato sauce	229 g can
10 oz. can	condensed tomato soup	268 g can
8 oz. can	mushrooms, drained	229 g can
	salt and pepper to taste	
16 oz. can	cream-style corn	489 g can
¼ lb.	shredded sharp Cheddar cheese	112 g

Spray a 3 qt. (3 L) microwave dish and lid with vegetable-oil spray. Add the broken spaghetti, water, and salad oil. Stir to moisten all the spaghetti. With the microwave on HIGH, cook, covered, for 5 minutes. Then stir and continue cooking on MEDIUM for 4 minutes. Drain thoroughly and rinse with cold running water. Combine the bacon, onion, and green pepper in a microwave dish. Cover with paper towels. With the microwave on HIGH, cook for 3 minutes, stirring at 1 minute intervals. Drain any grease from the dish. Stir in the tomato sauce, tomato soup, mushrooms, salt, and pepper. With the microwave on MEDIUM, cook for 2 minutes. Add the cooked spaghetti and corn, stirring to thoroughly mix. Top with the cheese. Cover with the microwave dish lid. Return to the microwave and cook on MEDIUM for 7 minutes or until the entire mixture is hot; stir after 3 minutes. Allow the mixture to stand for 5 minutes before serving.

Yield: 12 servings
Exchange, 1 serving: 2 bread, 1 fat
Calories, 1 serving: 193
Carbohydrates, 1 serving: 30

Mushroom Noodle Combo

1 qt.	extra-wide noodles	1 L
3 c.	water	750 mL
1 T.	low-calorie margarine	15 mL
1 c.	sliced mushrooms	250 mL
⅓ c.	chopped onions	90 mL
½ c.	cream of mushroom soup	125 mL
⅓ c.	skim milk	90 mL

Spray a 3 qt. (3 L) microwave dish and cover with vegetable-oil spray. Add the noodles and water. Stir to moisten all the noodles. With the microwave on HIGH, cook, covered, for 5 minutes. Stir and then return to the microwave and cook on MEDIUM for 5 more minutes. Drain thoroughly. Return the noodles to the microwave dish. Stir in the margarine, mushrooms, and onions. Combine the mushroom soup and milk in a bowl. Pour over the noodle mixture, stirring slightly. Return to the microwave and cook on MEDIUM for 3 minutes.

Yield: 20 servings
Exchange, 1 serving: 1½ bread
Calories, 1 serving: 105
Carbohydrates, 1 serving: 21

Dried Beef and Noodle Bake

1½ c.	water	375 mL
2 c.	macaroni	500 mL
½ c.	chopped dried beef	125 mL
¾ c.	chopped onion	190 mL
1 T.	low-calorie margarine	15 mL
1 c.	skim milk	250 mL
5 t.	all-purpose flour	25 mL
½ c.	shredded processed American cheese	125 mL

Combine the water and macaroni in a 2 qt. (2 L) microwave dish. Cover and cook in the microwave on HIGH for 10 minutes. Stir and turn the dish one-half rotation after 5 minutes. Drain thoroughly. Return the macaroni to the microwave dish and stir in the dried beef, onion, and margarine. Combine the milk and flour in a shaker or cup, blending thoroughly. Pour and blend it into the macaroni mixture. Cover with paper towels and cook on MEDIUM for 4 minutes. Sprinkle cheese over the top of the mixture. Cover loosely with paper towels, and cook on MEDIUM for 3 to 4 minutes or until the cheese is melted.

Yield: 12 servings
Exchange, 1 serving: 1 bread, ⅔ medium-fat meat
Calories, 1 serving: 137
Carbohydrates, 1 serving: 17

Meatless Lasagna

32 oz. jar	meatless spaghetti sauce	912 g jar
⅓ c.	grated Parmesan cheese	90 mL
2 c.	reduced-calorie ricotta cheese	500 mL
1 T.	parsley	15 mL
12	uncooked lasagna noodles	12
1 c.	shredded mozzarella cheese	250 mL
2 T.	Romano cheese	30 mL

Pour 1 c. (250 cm) of the spaghetti sauce into the bottom of a vegetable-oil-sprayed 13 × 9 in. (33 × 23 cm) microwave baking dish. Combine the Parmesan cheese, ricotta cheese, and parsley in a bowl. Place four uncooked lasagna noodles on top of the sauce. Layer with half of the ricotta cheese mixture. Sprinkle with a third of the mozzarella cheese. Repeat with a layer of ¾ c. sauce, four noodles, the remaining half of the ricotta cheese, and a third of the mozzarella cheese. Cover with the remaining four noodles, sauce, and mozzarella cheese. Then sprinkle the top with the Romano cheese. Cover with wax paper and cook with the microwave on HIGH for 15 minutes; rotate the dish one-quarter turn every 5 minutes. Continue cooking on MEDIUM for 20 minutes, rotating the dish one-quarter turn every 5 minutes. Remove the dish from the microwave and carefully remove the wax paper. Cover with aluminum foil and let stand for 15 to 20 minutes before serving.

Yield: 12 servings
Exchange, 1 serving: ½ bread, 1 high-fat meat
Calories, 1 serving: 137
Carbohydrates, 1 serving: 7

Spanish Vermicelli

1 c.	chopped onions	250 mL
28 oz. can	tomatoes	801 g can
½ c.	finely chopped green pepper	125 mL
½ t.	salt	2 mL
⅛ t.	ground cloves	½ mL
1	bay leaf	1
8 oz.	vermicelli noodles, cooked	229 g

Spray a 2 qt. (2 L) microwave dish and cover with vegetable-oil spray. And the onions, tomatoes, green pepper, salt, cloves, and bay leaf. Cover and cook with the microwave on HIGH for 1 minute, stir, and then continue cooking on MEDIUM for 4 minutes. Stir in the cooked vermicelli, re-cover, and return to the microwave. With the microwave on MEDIUM, cook 5 minutes, rotating the dish halfway through the cooking.

Yield: 12 servings
Exchange, 1 serving: 1 bread, ½ vegetable
Calories, 1 serving: 93
Carbohydrates, 1 serving: 18

Linguine with Clam Sauce

2 T.	olive oil	30 mL
1 clove	garlic, thinly sliced	1 clove
1 T.	freshly chopped parsley	15 mL
½ t.	oregano	2 mL
10 oz. can	baby clams, with juice	265 g can
8 oz.	linguine, cooked	229 g

Combine the olive oil and garlic in a large measuring cup. With the microwave on HIGH, cook, uncovered, for 3 minutes or until the garlic is slightly brown. Stir in the parsley, oregano, and clams with juice. Return to the microwave and cook on MEDIUM for 2 minutes. Serve over the hot cooked linguine.

Yield: 12 servings
Exchange, 1 serving: 1 bread, ½ fat
Calories, 1 serving: 101
Carbohydrates, 1 serving: 16

Shrimp Tetrazzini

7 oz. pkg.	spaghetti, cooked	210 g pkg.
1 c.	sliced mushrooms	250 mL
¼ c.	chopped green pepper	60 mL
¼ c.	chopped sweet red pepper	60 mL
2 T.	chopped onion	30 mL
¼ c.	all-purpose flour	60 mL
½ t.	salt	2 mL
dash	black pepper	dash
1 c.	skim milk	250 mL
1 c.	low-fat milk	250 mL
12 oz.	frozen shrimp, thawed	360 g

Prepare the spaghetti; then allow to cool completely under cool running water. Combine the mushrooms, peppers, and onion in a 2 qt. (2 L) microwave casserole or baking dish. Cover with a lid or plastic wrap. With the microwave on HIGH, cook for 3 minutes, stirring after 1 minute. Stir in the flour, salt, and pepper. Gradually add the skim milk and low-fat milk, stirring to blend completely. Return to the microwave, uncovered, and cook on HIGH for 4 to 5 minutes or until the mixture is thickened. Stir after 2 minutes—then, every minute. Stir in the shrimp and spaghetti. Heat, uncovered, for 7 minutes, stirring every 2 minutes. Remove the casserole from the microwave, and stir thoroughly. Taste for heat; if not serving temperature, return to the microwave and continue cooking on MEDIUM for 2 to 3 minutes.

Yield: 12 servings
Exchange, 1 serving: 1 bread, 1 lean meat, ⅓ low-fat milk
Calories, 1 serving: 140
Carbohydrates, 1 serving: 19

Creamy Chicken-and-Mushroom Noodle Dish

2 c.	water	500 mL
3 c.	noodles	750 mL
1 c.	chopped cooked chicken	250 mL
½ c.	sliced mushrooms	125 mL
3 T.	chopped celery	45 mL
1 T.	low-calorie margarine	15 mL
¾ c.	skim milk	190 mL
4 t.	all-purpose flour	20 mL
	salt and pepper	

Pour the water into a 2 qt. (2 L) casserole with a cover. Add the noodles and some salt as desired; then stir. Cover and cook with microwave on HIGH for 7 minutes. Add the chicken, mushrooms, and celery, stirring to mix. Cover and cook with the microwave on HIGH for 5 minutes. Stir the margarine into the mixture. Combine the milk and flour in a shaker or cup, blending thoroughly. Pour and stir it into the noodle mixture. Cover and cook with the microwave on HIGH for 2 minutes. Stir and allow to set for 3 to 4 minutes before serving. Add salt and pepper to taste.

Yield: 15 servings
Exchange, 1 serving: 1½ bread, ½ lean meat
Calories, 1 serving: 157
Carbohydrates, 1 serving: 23

Rice

Wild Rice

1 lb.	long-grain wild rice	500 g
1 qt.	water	1 L
	salt	

Combine the rice, water, and salt in a 3 qt. (3 L) casserole with a cover. With the microwave on HIGH, cook for 5 minutes. Stir to mix. Still on HIGH, cook for 5 minutes; then rotate the casserole one-quarter turn. Cook on MEDIUM for 10 minutes; then rotate one-quarter turn. Cook on HIGH for 5 more minutes. The rice should show the white kernel on the inside. Allow to set for 10 to 15 minutes before cooling.

To package for the freezer: Drain the rice in a strainer and cool it with running water. Allow to drain. Spoon 1 c. (250 mL) of the cooled rice into small freezer bags for future use.

Yield: ⅓ cup
Exchange, ⅓ cup (90 mL): 1 bread
Calories, ⅓ cup (90 mL): 83
Carbohydrates, ⅓ cup (90 mL): 15

Cheese and Rice

1 c.	uncooked rice	250 mL
	boiling water	
1 c.	skim milk	250 mL
½ c.	water	125 mL
½ c.	shredded American cheese	125 mL
1	egg, beaten	1

½ c.	finely chopped parsley	125 mL
½ c.	chopped onion	125 mL
2 T.	low-calorie margarine	30 mL

Place the rice in a large mixing bowl. Cover completely with boiling water. Cover with plastic wrap. Allow the rice to rest and steam for 20 minutes. Drain thoroughly. Rinse the rice with cold running water until completely cool. Drain. Combine the steamed rice and remaining ingredients in a greased 3 qt. (3 L) covered microwave dish. Stir to mix. With the microwave on MEDIUM, cook for 15 minutes or until the rice is tender and the liquid is absorbed (if needed, extra water may be added), stirring the mixture and rotating the dish every 3 to 4 minutes.

Yield: 12 servings
Exchange, 1 serving: ½ bread, ½ fat
Calories, 1 serving: 96
Carbohydrates, 1 serving: 13

Rice Skillet

1 c.	water	250 mL
½ c.	long-grain white rice	125 mL
	salt to taste	
½ c.	sliced celery	125 mL
¼ c.	chopped onion or chives	60 mL
1 c.	cooked wild rice	250 mL
1½ T.	soy sauce	21 mL

Combine the water, white rice, and salt to taste in a vegetable-oil-sprayed 10 in. (25 cm) pie plate. Stir to mix. Cover tightly with microwave plastic wrap. With the microwave on HIGH, cook for 3 minutes. Turn the dish one-half rotation. Cook on MEDIUM for 3 minutes. *Remove the plastic wrap very carefully—steam can burn.* Stir in the celery and onions. Cover with a new sheet of plastic wrap. With the microwave on MEDIUM, cook for 3 minutes. Remove the plastic wrap carefully, and stir in the wild rice and soy sauce. Re-cover with the plastic wrap, and cook for 2 minutes on MEDIUM.

Yield: 5 servings
Exchange, 1 serving: 1 bread
Calories, 1 serving: 78
Carbohydrates, 1 serving: 15

Plain Rice

1 c.	uncooked rice	250 mL
2 c.	water	500 mL
1 t.	vegetable oil	5 mL
dash	salt	dash

Combine all the ingredients in a 2 qt. (2 L) microwave casserole or baking dish. Cover with a lid or plastic wrap. With the microwave on HIGH, cook for 5 minutes. Stir and then rotate the dish one-quarter turn. Continue cooking on MEDIUM for 10 minutes or until most of the water is absorbed. Keeping the dish covered, allow the rice to absorb the moisture for 10 minutes.

Yield: 6 servings
Exchange, 1 serving: 1 bread
Calories, 1 serving: 80
Carbohydrates, 1 serving: 17

Orange Rice

1 c.	uncooked rice	250 mL
1 c.	water	250 mL
1 c.	orange juice	250 mL
1 t.	reduced-calorie margarine	5 mL
dash	salt	dash
1 T.	fresh grated orange rind	15 mL
½ c.	fresh orange sections	125 mL

Combine the rice, water, orange juice, margarine, and salt in a 2 qt. (2 L) microwave casserole or baking dish. Cover with a lid or plastic wrap. With the microwave on HIGH, cook for 5 minutes. Stir in the orange rind and rotate the dish one-quarter turn. Continue cooking on MEDIUM for 10 minutes or until most of the water is absorbed. Keep covered and allow the rice to absorb the moisture for 10 minutes. Just before serving, add the orange sections and toss to mix.

Yield: 6 servings
Exchange, 1 serving: 1 bread, 1 fruit
Calories, 1 serving: 104
Carbohydrates, 1 serving: 30

Pilaf

1 T.	low-calorie margarine	15 mL
¾ c.	chicken broth	190 mL
⅔ c.	beef broth	180 mL
1½ c.	uncooked long-grain rice	375 mL

Melt the margarine in a 3 qt. (3 L) covered microwave dish. And the broths. With the microwave on HIGH, cook for 2 minutes or until the broth is bubbling. Stir in the rice. Cook, covered, on MEDIUM for 15 minutes or until the liquid is absorbed—stirring the mixture and rotating the dish every 3 to 4 minutes.

Yield: 8 servings
Exchange, 1 serving: 1 bread
Calories, 1 serving: 82
Carbohydrates, 1 serving: 16

Spanish Rice

1½ c.	chopped onions	375 mL
28 oz. can	tomatoes	801 g can
½ c.	finely chopped green pepper	125 mL
½ t.	salt	2 mL
dash	ground cloves	dash
1	bay leaf	1
1 c.	uncooked long-grain white rice	250 mL

Spray a 3 qt. (3 L) microwave dish and cover with vegetable-oil spray. Add the onions, tomatoes, green pepper, salt, cloves, and bay leaf. Cover and cook with the microwave on HIGH for 1 minute. Stir and then continue cooking on MEDIUM for 4 minutes. Stir in the rice, re-cover, and return to the microwave. Cook on MEDIUM for 10 minutes, rotating the dish and stirring every 2 minutes.

Yield: 6 servings
Exchange, 1 serving: 1 bread, 1 vegetable
Calories, 1 serving: 115
Carbohydrates, 1 serving: 21

Vegetables

Green Beans and Ham

1 T.	reduced-calorie margarine	15 mL
⅓ c.	cubed cooked ham	
1 clove	garlic, chopped	
16 oz. can	French-style green beans	489 g can
	salt and pepper to taste	
1	tomato, cut in 8 wedges	1

Combine the margarine, ham, and chopped garlic in a medium-sized microwave dish with a cover. With the microwave on MEDIUM, cook for 3 minutes. Drain the green beans and toss them with the ham mixture. Add salt and pepper to taste. Cover and continue cooking on MEDIUM for 2½ minutes. Remove the cover, and top the mixture with the tomato wedges. Cover lightly with wax paper. With the microwave on MEDIUM, cook for 1 minute.

Yield: 4 servings
Exchange, 1 serving: 1 vegetable
Calories, 1 serving: 28
Carbohydrates, 1 serving: 6

Vegetable Supreme

9 oz. pkg.	frozen French-style green beans	239 g pkg.
10 oz. pkg.	frozen peas	285 g pkg.
10 oz. pkg.	frozen lima beans	285 g pkg.
½ c.	reduced-calorie salad dressing	125 mL

2 T.	lemon juice	30 mL
3 T.	finely chopped onions	45 mL
2 t.	Worcestershire sauce	10 mL
1 t.	Dijon mustard	5 mL
¼ t.	garlic salt	1 mL

Thaw, drain, and then combine the vegetables in a microwave dish with a cover. With the microwave on MEDIUM, cook for 4 minutes. Set aside. Combine the salad dressing, lemon juice, onion, Worcestershire sauce, mustard, and garlic salt in a microwave dish with a cover. Stir to blend. Cover and cook on MEDIUM LOW for 2 minutes. Stir and then, if the mixture is not warm, return to the microwave and cook 1 more minute. Pour the sauce over the vegetables. Cover and cook on MEDIUM LOW for 3 minutes, stirring after each minute.

Yield: 8 servings
Exchange, 1 serving: 1 bread
Calories, 1 serving: 72
Carbohydrates, 1 serving: 12

Eggplant and Onion with Cheese

1½ lbs.	eggplant	1½ kg
½ lb.	mushrooms	250 g
½ lb.	mozzarella cheese	500
16 oz. jar	spaghetti sauce	446 g jar
½ c.	grated Parmesan cheese	125 mL

Cut the eggplant, mushrooms, and mozzarella cheese into thin slices. Grease a 13 × 9 in. (33 × 23 cm) microwave pan. Place a layer of half of the eggplant, mushrooms, and cheese on the bottom of the pan. Cover with half of the sauce. Repeat the layer, topping with the sauce; then sprinkle with the Parmesan cheese. Cover the pan with wax paper. With the microwave on HIGH, cook for 5 minutes. Rotate the pan one-quarter turn. Continue cooking on MEDIUM HIGH for 10 minutes, rotating the pan one-quarter turn every 5 minutes.

Yield: 8 servings
Exchange, 1 serving: ½ vegetable, 1 high-fat meat
Calories, 1 serving: 125
Carbohydrates, 1 serving: 5

Spaghetti Squash, Italian Style

3 lb.	spaghetti squash	1½ kg
¼ c.	reduced-calorie Italian dressing	60 mL
2 T.	fresh snipped parsley	30 mL

Wash the squash; then cut off both ends and prick the outer skin. Wrap in plastic wrap. With the microwave on HIGH, cook for 6 to 7 minutes or until the squash is soft. Carefully remove the plastic wrap. Cut the squash in half lengthwise. Remove the seeds. Then remove the flesh by scraping the insides of the squash lengthwise with the tongs of a fork. (Spaghetti squash has thread-like strands.) Place the squash in a bowl. Toss with the Italian dressing. Cover tightly with plastic wrap. Return to the microwave and cook on MEDIUM for 2 minutes. Just before serving, sprinkle with parsley.

Yield: 8 servings
Exchange, 1 serving: 1 vegetable
Calories, 1 serving: 27
Carbohydrates, 1 serving: 6

Cabbage with Dijon Sauce

1 small head	cabbage, cut in four wedges	1 small head
2 T.	finely chopped onion or chives	30 mL
1 T.	water	15 mL
2 t.	all-purpose flour	10 mL
1 c.	skim milk	250 mL
1 T.	Dijon mustard	15 mL

Place the cabbage wedges in a 10 in. (25 cm) pie pan. Add a small amount of water to the pan and cover tightly with plastic wrap. With the microwave on HIGH, cook for 5 to 6 minutes or until the cabbage is tender-crisp. Remove from the microwave and allow to rest, covered, while making the sauce. Now, combine the onion and 1 T. (15 mL) of water in a mixing bowl or measuring cup. Cook, uncovered, on HIGH for 2 minutes. Sprinkle the flour over the onions and stir. Slowly add the milk to the onion, stirring to blend. Stir in the mustard. Return the bowl to the microwave and cook on HIGH for 5 minutes or until the sauce reaches desired consistency, stirring occasionally. Remove the plastic wrap from the cabbage wedges, drain any excess water, and then pour the sauce over the cabbage. Return the cabbage to the microwave, and cook on MEDIUM for 1 to 2 minutes. Serve hot.

Yield: 4 servings
Exchange, 1 serving: 1 vegetable, ¼ skim milk
Calories, 1 serving: 47
Carbohydrates, 1 serving: 9

Cooked Vegetable Salad

1 c.	frozen carrots, thawed	250 mL
1 c.	frozen snap green beans, thawed	250 mL
1 c.	frozen cauliflower, thawed	250 mL
½	red pepper, cut in strips	½
½ c.	sliced mushrooms	125 mL
½ c.	reduced-calorie salad dressing	125 mL
	onion salt	
	black pepper	

Combine the vegetables in a covered microwave dish. With the microwave on MEDIUM, cook for 7 to 8 minutes, rotating the dish one-fourth turn after 4 minutes. Allow the vegetables to rest for 2 minutes; then drain any excess moisture. Fold in the salad dressing and the desired amount of onion salt and black pepper. Cover and chill at least 2 hours. Drain just before serving.

Yield: 6 servings
Exchange, 1 serving: 1 vegetable
Calories, 1 serving: 27
Carbohydrates, 1 serving: 5

Creamed Corn

16 oz. can	whole-kernel corn	424 g can
1	egg	1
½ c.	skim milk	125 mL
¼ c.	unsalted saltine cracker crumbs	60 mL
2 t.	reduced-calorie margarine	10 mL
½ t.	salt	2 mL
dash each	black pepper, nutmeg	dash each

Drain the corn. Pour half of the corn in a blender. Add the egg and blend on HIGH until the corn is almost a puree. Combine the remaining whole-kernel corn, corn puree, and other remaining ingredients in a 1 qt. (1 L) lightly greased casserole or microwave bowl. Stir to blend. Allow to stand for 3 minutes. Cover with a lid or wax paper. With the microwave on MEDIUM, cook for 6 to 7 minutes or until the mixture is set.

Yield: 6 servings
Exchange, 1 serving: 1 bread
Calories, 1 serving: 92
Carbohydrates, 1 serving: 17

Zucchini Casserole

1 lb.	zucchini	500 g
1 clove	garlic	1 clove
2 t.	reduced-calorie margarine	10 mL
2 slices	white bread	2 slices
½ t.	oregano	2 mL
½ t.	sage	2 mL
	salt and pepper	

Wash the zucchini; then cut off the ends and prick the surface in several places with a sharp fork or knife. Wrap the zucchini in plastic wrap. With the microwave on HIGH, cook for 5 minutes, rotating the zucchini once during cooking. Carefully remove the plastic wrap. Cut the zucchini in half lengthwise, remove the seeds, and scoop out the pulp. Place the pulp in a microwave dish. Next, thinly slice the garlic clove.

Combine the garlic slices and margarine in a measuring cup. With the microwave on HIGH, cook for 1 minute. Add the garlic and the remaining ingredients to the zucchini pulp. Stir to mix thoroughly. Cover and return to the microwave, cooking on MEDIUM for 3 minutes or until hot.

Yield: 4 servings
Exchange, 1 serving: 1 vegetable, ¼ bread
Calories, 1 serving: 43
Carbohydrates, 1 serving: 9

Mandarin Squash

2 lbs.	summer squash*	1 kg
1 T.	reduced-calorie margarine	15 mL
8 oz. can	mandarin orange sections	212 g can
1 T.	granulated brown sugar replacement	15 mL
¼ t.	nutmeg	1 mL

*Summer squash have a thin skin and light color. Examples are scallop or pattypan, zucchini, yellow crooked neck or straight neck, and chayote.

Peel and cut the squash into lengthwise strips. Place them in a 2 qt. (2 L) baking dish with a cover. Dot with the margarine. With the microwave on HIGH, cook for 6 minutes or until the squash is tender; rotate the dish twice during cooking. Allow the squash to rest, covered, while making the sauce. Drain the liquid from the mandarin orange sections into a medium-sized bowl; then add the brown sugar replacement and nutmeg. With the microwave on HIGH, cook for 1 minute or until boiling. Stir the orange sections into the liquid. Drain any excess liquid from the squash. Now, pour the mandarin orange sauce over the squash. Serve hot.

Yield: 6 servings
Exchange, 1 serving: 1 vegetable, ¼ fruit
Calories, 1 serving: 45
Carbohydrates, 1 serving: 9

Red Cabbage

2 qts.	shredded red cabbage	2 L	
1 c.	water	250 mL	
1 T.	instant chicken broth mix	15 mL	
1	apple, peeled and chopped	1	
1 T.	red wine vinegar	15 mL	
2 t.	granulated sugar replacement	10 mL	
1 in.	cinnamon stick	2.5 cm	
2	whole cloves	2	

Combine the cabbage, water, and chicken broth mix in a large microwave bowl or casserole. Cover tightly with a lid or plastic wrap. With the microwave on HIGH, cook for 6 to 7 minutes. Add the remaining ingredients, and continue cooking on HIGH for 7 or 8 minutes or until the cabbage is tender. Transfer with a slotted spoon to a serving dish. Remove the cinnamon stick and cloves.

Yield: 6 servings
Exchange, 1 serving: 1 vegetable
Calories, 1 serving: 28
Carbohydrates, 1 serving: 7

Broccoli Supreme

10 oz. pkg.	frozen broccoli, thawed	285 g pkg.
¼ c.	chopped chives or green onions	60 mL
¼ c.	chopped mushrooms	60 mL
1 T.	reduced-calorie margarine	15 mL

Combine all the ingredients in a microwave serving bowl or other microwave dish. Stir to mix. Cover with wax paper. With the microwave on MEDIUM, cook for 3 minutes. Stir and then turn the dish one-quarter rotation. Continue cooking on MEDIUM for 4 to 5 minutes or until the mushrooms and onions are tender.

Yield: 4 servings
Exchange, 1 serving: 1 vegetable
Calories, 1 serving: 24
Carbohydrates, 1 serving: 4

Spiced Carrots

4	carrots	4
1 T.	water	15 mL
2 t.	reduced-calorie margarine	10 mL
1 T.	fresh snipped parsley	15 mL
1 T.	cream sherry	15 mL
¼ t.	cinnamon	1 mL
	salt and pepper	

Peel the carrots and then cut them into julienne strips. Combine the carrot strips and water in a bowl. Cover tightly with plastic wrap. With the microwave on HIGH, cook for 3 minutes. Carefully remove the plastic wrap. Add the margarine and toss to melt. Sprinkle with the remaining ingredients.

Yield: 4 servings
Exchange, 1 serving: ½ bread
Calories, 1 serving: 32
Carbohydrates, 1 serving: 7

Easy Fresh Vegetables

1 c.	sliced carrots	250 mL
1 c.	sliced celery	250 mL
½ c.	onions, cut in large pieces	125 mL
2 t.	water	10 mL
2 t.	reduced-calorie margarine	10 mL
	salt and pepper	

Combine the vegetables and water in a serving dish, and cover with plastic wrap. With the microwave on HIGH, cook for 5 to 6 minutes or until the carrots are crisp-tender. Carefully remove the plastic wrap, and top the vegetables with the margarine, salt, and pepper. Re-cover with the plastic wrap, and cook on HIGH for 2 minutes.

Yield: 4 servings
Exchange, 1 serving: 1 vegetable
Calories, 1 serving: 23
Carbohydrates, 1 serving: 5

Winter Squash

There are many types of winter squash. They have a tough, coarse outer skin and usually a sweet, orange interior. The common winter squash are acorn, butternut, Hubbard, turban, and pumpkin. The tough outer skin, or rind, is usually very difficult to cut. If your squash is small enough to fit in your microwave, the following is the easiest cooking method. First, wash the outer rind thoroughly. Prick the outer rind with a sharp knife or poultry pin in many places; this pricking allows the steam to escape. Wrap the wet squash in plastic wrap. With the microwave on HIGH or MEDIUM, cook until the outer rind is soft. Then cut and cook according to any further directions.

Easy Acorn Squash

1	acorn squash	1
2 T.	granulated brown sugar replacement	30 mL
2 t.	reduced-calorie margarine	10 mL

Wash the outside of the acorn squash, prick the surface of the squash in several places with a sharp fork or knife, and then wrap the squash in plastic wrap. With the microwave on HIGH, cook the squash for 7 to 8 minutes or until it feels slightly soft. Carefully remove the plastic wrap. Cut the squash in half and remove the seeds. Place the squash, with the cut side up, on a baking plate. Sprinkle each half with 1 T. (15 mL) of the granulated brown sugar replacement and add 1 t. (5 mL) of the margarine to the middle of each half. Cover with plastic wrap and continue cooking on HIGH for 3 to 4 minutes or until the squash is tender and hot. Cut each half in half to serve.

Yield: 4 servings
Exchange, 1 serving: ½ bread
Calories, 1 serving: 43
Carbohydrates, 1 serving: 8

Winter Squash with Apples

2 c.	sliced peeled apples	500 mL
1 t.	cinnamon	5 mL
½ t.	nutmeg	2 mL
¼ t.	ginger	1 mL
3 T.	granulated sugar replacement	45 mL
1 qt.	mashed cooked winter squash	1 L

Combine the apples and spices in a 2 qt. (2 L) casserole or bowl. Cover with a lid or plastic wrap. With the microwave on MEDIUM, cook for 4 to 5 minutes or until the apples are crisp-tender. Stir in the sugar replacement and mashed squash. Return to the microwave and cook on MEDIUM for 10 minutes or until hot.

Yield: 6 servings
Exchange, 1 serving: ½ bread, 1 fruit
Calories, 1 serving: 97
Carbohydrates, 1 serving: 16

Winter Squash Casserole

2 c.	mashed cooked winter squash	500 mL
3 T.	dietetic maple syrup	45 mL
1 T.	yellow mustard	15 mL
1	egg, slightly beaten	1
	salt and pepper	

Combine all the ingredients in a mixing bowl. Beat to blend. Grease a 1½ qt. (1½ L) casserole with vegetable-oil spray. Transfer the squash mixture to the casserole. Cook, uncovered, in the microwave for 4 minutes on MEDIUM LOW. Then rotate the dish one-quarter turn, and continue cooking on MEDIUM for 5 to 6 minutes or until the mixture is hot.

Yield: 4 servings
Exchange, 1 serving: ½ bread, ¼ high-fat meat
Calories, 1 serving: 60
Carbohydrates, 1 serving: 8

Beef

Pepper Steak

¾ lb.	boneless beef round steak	375 g
2 T.	corn oil	30 mL
1 medium	onion	1 medium
1	green pepper	1
1	tomato	1
1 clove	garlic, minced	1 clove
2 t.	cornstarch	10 mL
⅓ c.	cold water	90 mL
1 T.	soy sauce	15 mL

Chill the steak thoroughly; then slice it into very thin strips. Heat the oil in the bottom of a 10 in. (25 cm) pie plate. Add the steak strips and cook on MEDIUM in the microwave for 3 to 4 minutes, stirring every minute. Remove the steak from the plate. Clean the vegetables, and cut them into medium-sized chunks. Place the vegetables and the garlic in the pie plate, and cover with plastic wrap. With the microwave on HIGH, cook for 3 minutes. Remove the vegetables. Combine the cornstarch, cold water, and soy sauce in a small mixing bowl; then stir to blend. Pour into the pie plate. With the microwave on MEDIUM, cook for 1 minute; then stir. Return both the meat and the vegetables to the pie plate, and cover. With the microwave on MEDIUM, cook for 2 to 3 minutes, stirring every 60 seconds until the mixture thickens.

Yield: 8 servings
Exchange, 1 serving: 1 medium-fat meat
Calories, 1 serving: 89
Carbohydrates, 1 serving: 2

Spicy Meatballs

¾ lb.	lean ground beef	375 g
1 c.	grated raw potatoes	250 mL
1 t.	salt	5 mL
3 T.	Pace hot picante sauce	45 mL
4 t.	all-purpose flour	20 mL

Combine all the ingredients and mix them thoroughly. Form into 16 small meatballs. Place the meatballs on the bottom of a 13 × 9 in. (33 × 23 cm) baking dish. Cover with wax paper. With the microwave on HIGH, cook for 3 minutes. Carefully remove the meatballs, and drain any liquid from the bottom of the dish. Return the meatballs to the dish by turning them over. Add ⅓ c. (90 mL) of water to the dish. Cover the plastic wrap. With the microwave on MEDIUM, cook for 4 minutes. Before serving, allow meatballs to set 5 minutes, covered with plastic wrap.

Yield: 16 servings
Exchange, 1 serving: ½ medium-fat meat
Calories, 1 serving: 41
Carbohydrates, 1 serving: 2

Beef Blade Steak

1½ lbs.	boneless beef chuck blade steak	¾ kg
1 clove	garlic, minced	1 clove
	salt and pepper to taste	

Slice the blade steak into six equal slices about ¾ in. (2 cm) thick. With the back of a spoon, rub the minced garlic on both sides of each steak slice. Place in a large, shallow microwave pan or 10 in. (23 cm) pie pan. Cover with two paper towels. With the microwave on HIGH, cook for 5 minutes. Remove the paper towels and discard. Turn the steaks over. Cover the clean paper towels, and cook on MEDIUM for 5 minutes or until the steaks are done. Add salt and pepper to taste.

Yield: 6 servings
Exchange, 1 serving: 1¾ high-fat meat
Calories, 1 serving: 185
Carbohydrates, 1 serving: negligible

Beef Roast with Parsley and Garlic

3 lb.	beef eye of round, trimmed	1½ kg
3 sprigs	fresh parsley, coarsely chopped	3 sprigs
2 cloves	garlic, thinly sliced	2 cloves
	salt and pepper	

Make six 3 in. (7.5 cm)-deep and ¾ in. (2 cm)-wide slits in the top of the roast. Use the handle of a spoon to stuff one third of the chopped parsley in the first slit, and one third of the sliced garlic in second slit. Repeat stuffing slits, alternating the parsley with the garlic. Wrap the roast with a string or use toothpicks to hold the shape. Sprinkle with salt and pepper. Place the roast on a roast rack in a microwave baking pan, and cover with wax paper. With the microwave on MEDIUM HIGH, cook for 15 minutes. Turn the roast over, cover with wax paper, and continue cooking 15 minutes longer. Allow the roast to rest 10 minutes before serving.

Yield: 20 servings
Exchange, 1 serving: 1¼ medium-fat meat
Calories, 1 serving: 92
Carbohydrates, 1 serving: negligible

Swiss Liver

1 lb.	calves' liver	500 g
3 T.	corn oil	45 mL
3 T.	chopped onion	45 mL
2 T.	chopped fresh parsley	30 mL
½ c.	reduced-calorie plain yogurt	125 mL

Cut the liver into thin strips. With the microwave on HIGH, heat the oil in the bottom of a 10 in. (25 cm) pie plate for 2 to 3 minutes or until it's hot and bubbly. Add the liver strips, onion, and parsley. With the microwave still on HIGH, cook for 5 to 7 minutes; stir or toss to mix every minute. (The liver should be pink in the middle—it should not be overcooked.) Stir the yogurt into the pan drippings just before serving.

Yield: 8 servings
Exchange, 1 serving: 1 high-fat meat
Calories, 1 serving: 135
Carbohydrates, 1 serving: negligible

Mushroom Meatloaf

1 lb.	lean ground beef	500 g
2.5 oz. pkg.	dry mushroom soup mix	71 g pkg.
½ c.	oatmeal	500 mL
1	egg	1
¼ c.	chopped chives or onion	60 mL
¼ c.	water	60 mL

Combine all the ingredients in a large bowl, and mix thoroughly. Form the mixture into a ball-like mound in the bottom of an 8 in. (20 cm) glass pie plate. Cover with plastic wrap. With the microwave on MEDIUM, cook for 12 to 15 minutes, turning the dish one-half rotation every 4 to 5 minutes.

Yield: 6 servings
Exchange, 1 serving: 1 medium-fat meat, ¾ bread
Calories, 1 serving: 156
Carbohydrates, 1 serving: 12

Creamed Dried Beef

4 oz.	dried beef	120 g
1 T.	reduced-calorie margarine	15 mL
2 T.	all-purpose flour	30 mL
1 c.	skim milk	250 mL
½ t.	Worcestershire sauce	2 mL

Shred or tear the dried beef into small pieces. Melt the margarine in a 1 qt. (1 L) microwave dish or casserole with a cover. Add the dried beef, cover, and cook on MEDIUM in the microwave for 2 minutes. Combine the flour, milk, and Worcestershire sauce in a mixing bowl. Stir to thoroughly blend. Pour over the dried beef. Cook, uncovered, on MEDIUM in the microwave for 10 to 12 minutes or until the sauce is of desired thickness; while cooking, stir every 3 minutes.

Yield: 4 servings
Exchange, 1 serving: 1 lean meat, ⅔ skim milk
Calories, 1 serving: 103
Carbohydrates, 1 serving: 9

Boiled Beef with Vegetables

1 lb.	lean beef chuck roast, cubed	500 g
1 qt.	boiling water	1 L
1 t.	salt	5 mL
3	leeks, sliced	3
2	carrots, sliced	2
1	onion, cut in eighths	1
1	turnip, sliced	1
1 sprig	parsley, chopped	1 sprig
4 medium	potatoes, sliced	4

Combine the beef cubes, boiling water, and salt in large microwave soup pot or 4 qt. covered casserole. With the microwave on HIGH, cook, covered, for 5 minutes; then reduce the heat to MEDIUM and cook 5 more minutes. Add the vegetables. With the microwave on MEDIUM, cook 20 to 25 minutes longer or until the vegetables are done.

Yield: 4 servings
Exchange, 1 serving: 2⅓ medium-fat meat, 1 bread
Calories, 1 serving: 265
Carbohydrates, 1 serving: 17

Royal Pot Roast

2 lbs.	lean beef pot roast	1 kg
1 t.	salt	5 mL
½ t.	allspice	2 mL
dash	black pepper	dash
2 T.	brandy	30 mL
1	onion, sliced	1
1	bay leaf	1
3 T.	hot water	45 mL
1 T.	white vinegar	15 mL
1 T.	molasses	15 mL
½ t.	anchovy paste	2 mL

Arrange the roast on a roast rack in a large microwave pan. Combine the salt, allspice, and black pepper in a small bowl. Rub this mixture onto all sides of the roast. Cook, uncovered, in the microwave on HIGH for 8 minutes. Turn the roast over and continue cooking for 5 minutes. Remove from the microwave. Remove the roast rack from the pan; then return the roast to the pan. Pour the brandy over the hot surface of the roast and flame. Add the onion slices and bay leaf. Combine the remaining ingredients in a bowl, stirring to mix. Pour over the roast. Cover with a lid or plastic wrap. Return to the microwave and continue cooking on MEDIUM for 15 to 20 minutes or until the roast is done, turning the pan a quarter rotation and basting with pan juices every 5 minutes. Allow the roast to rest at least 10 minutes before carving.

Yield: 10 servings
Exchange, 1 serving: 1½ high-fat meat
Calories, 1 serving: 148
Carbohydrates, 1 serving: negligible

Angel Steak

2 lbs.	beef round steak, cut ¾ in. (2 cm) thick	1 kg
¼ c.	all-purpose flour	60 mL
¼ c.	cracker crumbs	60 mL
1½ oz. pkg.	taco seasoning mix	42 g pkg.
2 slices	bacon, cut in half	2 slices
1	onion, thinly sliced	1
½ c.	water	125 mL

Cut the round steak into six equal portions. Mix the flour, cracker crumbs, and taco mix in a bowl. Pound this taco mixture into the steak on both sides. Set aside. Arrange the bacon pieces on the bottom of a 8 in. (20 cm)-square microwave dish. Cover with paper towels. With the microwave on HIGH, cook for 2 minutes. Remove the bacon pieces. Pour off the excess bacon grease. Arrange the steak on the bottom of the pan. Add the bacon, onion, and water. Cover with wax paper. With the microwave on MEDIUM, cook for 10 to 12 minutes, rotating the dish a quarter turn every 3 minutes. Allow the steak to rest 5 minutes before serving.

Yield: 6 servings
Exchange, 1 serving: 3½ medium-fat meat, 1 bread
Calories, 1 serving: 343
Carbohydrates, 1 serving: 16

Beef with Red Wine

3 lbs.	rolled beef rump roast	1½ kg
1 c.	dry red wine	250 mL
	salt and pepper to taste	

Arrange the roast on a roasting rack in a large microwave pan. Cook in the microwave, uncovered, on HIGH for 8 minutes. Turn the roast over and continue cooking on HIGH for another 8 minutes. Baste the roast with the wine. Cover with plastic wrap. With the microwave on MEDIUM, cook for 15 minutes longer—turning the roast over and basting it with wine every 5 minutes. Allow the roast to rest at least 10 minutes before carving. Baste with pan juices just before serving. Add salt and pepper to taste.

Yield: 20 servings
Exchange, 1 serving: 1¼ medium-fat meat
Calories, 1 serving: 93
Carbohydrates, 1 serving: negligible

Lean & Free Sirloin Kabobs

¾ c.	reduced-salt soy sauce	
¼ c.	dietetic maple syrup	60 mL
1 lb.	Lean & Free beef sirloin	500 g
	(cut in 1 in. (2.5 cm) cubes)	
24	pineapple chunks, in their own juice	24
1	green pepper, cut in squares	1

Combine the soy sauce and dietetic maple syrup in a bowl. Add the sirloin cubes and stir to coat. Cover and marinate 1 hour. Remove the sirloin cubes, and reserve the marinade. Alternately place the sirloin cubes, pineapple chunks, and green pepper squares on a wooden or plastic skewer. Place the kabobs in an 8 in. (20 cm)-square microwave or glass baking dish. Brush with the marinade. Cover with wax paper. With the microwave on HIGH, cook for 4 minutes. Rotate the dish a quarter turn and brush with the marinade. Re-cover with wax paper. Continue cooking in the microwave on MEDIUM for 4 minutes. Allow to rest 4 minutes before serving. Brush with the remaining marinade just before serving.

Yield: 8 servings
Exchange, 1 serving: 1 medium-fat meat
Calories, 1 serving: 80
Carbohydrates, 1 serving: 1

Beef and Pork Dish

½ lb.	lean ground beef	250 g
½ lb.	lean ground pork	250 g
2 c.	water	500 mL
6 oz. can	tomato paste	180 g can
4	tomatoes, diced	4
3	potatoes, diced	3
3	green onions, thinly sliced	3
2	jalapeño peppers, chopped	2
⅓ c.	raisins	90 mL
2 cloves	garlic, minced	2 cloves
2 t.	salt	10 mL
¼ t.	black pepper	1 mL
¼ t.	oregano	1 mL

Combine all the ingredients in a large microwave soup pot or casserole. Stir to blend completely. Cover and cook with the microwave on HIGH for 3 minutes or just until the mixture begins to boil. Reduce the heat to LOW and continue cooking for 7 to 8 minutes or until the potatoes are tender.

Yield: 5 servings
Exchange, 1 serving: 1½ medium-fat meat, 1 bread, ½ fruit
Calories, 1 serving: 284
Carbohydrates, 1 serving: 22

Beefsteak and Oysters

1 lb.	boneless beef sirloin steak	500 g
8 oz. can	whole oysters, drained	225 g can
2 t.	reduced-calorie margarine	10 mL
	salt and pepper	

Slice the meat across the grain into ¼ in. (8 mm) strips. Place the steak strips in a microwave casserole with a lid. Cover with the lid or use wax paper. With the microwave on HIGH, cook for 30 seconds. Stir the meat strips. Pour the oysters over the top of the steak. Add the margarine and salt and pepper. With the microwave on HIGH, cook for 2 or 3 minutes or until the oysters are done—the oysters will plump and begin to curl at the edges.

Yield: 8 servings
Exchange, 1 serving: 1⅓ medium-fat meat
Calories, 1 serving: 115
Carbohydrates, 1 serving: negligible

Meatballs for Supper

1 lb.	lean ground beef	500 g
1 c.	shredded raw potatoes	250 mL
1	onion, chopped	1
1	egg	1
1 T.	parsley flakes	15 mL
½ t.	salt	2 mL
¼ t.	black pepper	1 mL
2 c.	water	500 mL
1½ T.	instant beef broth mix	21 mL
2 T.	cornstarch	30 mL
2 T.	cold water	30 mL

Combine the ground beef, potatoes, onion, egg, parsley flakes, salt, and pepper in a mixing bowl. Stir with a spoon or mix with your hands until thoroughly blended. Form the mixture into 12 balls. Set aside. Combine the 2 c. (500 mL) of water with the beef broth mix in a 2 qt. (2 L) microwave casserole dish. With the microwave on HIGH, cook for 3 to 5 minutes or just until boiling. Add the beef balls. Then cover and continue cooking with the microwave on MEDIUM for 8 minutes. Combine the cornstarch and the 2 T. (30 mL) of cold water in a cup. Pour into the beef ball mixture and stir to blend. Return the uncovered casserole to the microwave. Stirring occasionally, continue cooking on ME-DIUM for 3 to 4 minutes or until the mixture is thickened.

Yield: 8 servings
Exchange, 1 serving: 1 high-fat meat, ¼ bread
Calories, 1 serving: 121
Carbohydrates, 1 serving: 4

Stuffed Rolled Beef

1 lb.	boneless beef round steak	500 g
¼ c.	lemon juice	60 mL
2 T.	soy sauce	30 mL
2 cloves	garlic, minced	2 cloves
½ c.	canned cream of mushroom soup, undiluted	125 mL
4 slices	thin-sliced white bread	4 slices
2	hard-boiled eggs	2
8 oz. can	tomato sauce	240 g can
1 c.	water	250 mL

Chill or slightly freeze the round steak. Remove any excess fat. Using the edge of a plate or a meat tenderizer, pound the steak until it is ¼ in. (8 mm) thick. Lay the steak out flat, and spread with lemon juice, soy sauce, and garlic. Allow to rest for 4 to 5 minutes. Spread with the mushroom soup. Lay the bread in a single layer on top of the mushroom soup. Crumble the hard-boiled eggs over the top. Start at one end and roll up jelly-roll style. Tie with string or secure the ends and seam tightly with toothpicks. Place the beef roll in the bottom of a shallow microwave or glass baking dish. Blend the tomato sauce and water together; then pour over the beef roll. Cover with wax paper. With the microwave on HIGH, cook for 5 minutes. Baste the beef roll with the sauce. Rotate the dish a quarter turn. Continue cooking on MEDIUM for 15 to 20 minutes or until the meat is fork-tender, basting and rotating the dish every 5 minutes.

Yield: 10 servings
Exchange, 1 serving: 1 medium-fat meat, ½ bread, ½ vegetable
Calories, 1 serving: 127
Carbohydrates, 1 serving: 11

Italian Meat Sauce

1 c.	chopped onion	250 mL
1 lb.	lean ground beef	500 g
1 c.	sliced mushrooms	250 mL
2 cloves	garlic, sliced	2 cloves
32 oz. jar	spaghetti sauce	907 g jar

Place the chopped onions in a 4 qt. (4 L) microwave casserole or glass bowl. Cover with a lid or plastic wrap. With the microwave on HIGH, cook for 2 minutes. Crumble half of the ground beef into the onions, stir, and add half of the mushrooms and the sliced garlic. Cover and cook on HIGH for 3 minutes, stirring to break up the meat. Crumble and add the remaining meat and mushrooms. Cover and continue cooking on HIGH for three minutes, stirring to break up the meat. Now, pour in the spaghetti sauce. Cover and cook on MEDIUM for 5 to 6 minutes or until hot. Serve over noodles, bread, potatoes, or rice.

Yield: 10 servings
Exchange, 1 serving (only meat sauce): 1 medium-fat meat, ½ vegetable
Calories, 1 serving (only meat sauce): 87
Carbohydrates, 1 serving (only meat sauce): 2

Corned Beef and Cabbage

3 lb.	corned beef brisket	1½ kg
2 c.	hot water	500 mL
1 large	cabbage	1 large

Place the brisket in a 4 qt. (4 L) microwave casserole or baking dish. Add the hot water. Cover with a lid or plastic wrap. With the microwave on HIGH, cook for 25 minutes. Turn the meat over, re-cover, and continue cooking on MEDIUM for 30 minutes. Clean the cabbage and then cut it into 10 wedges. Place the wedges around the brisket. Cover and continue cooking on MEDIUM for 30 minutes more, rotating the dish a quarter turn every 10 minutes.

Yield: 20 servings
Exchange, 1 serving: 1½ high-fat meat, ¼ vegetable
Calories, 1 serving: 161
Carbohydrates, 1 serving: 1

Pork

Pork Chops Smothered with Apples

6	½ in. (½₅ cm) center-cut pork loin chops	6
¼ t.	salt	1 mL
¼ t.	sage	1 mL
3	tart apples	3
⅓ c.	sultana raisins	90 mL
3 T.	dietetic maple syrup	45 mL
1½ c.	water	375 mL
3 T.	all-purpose flour	45 mL
1 T.	cider vinegar	15 mL

Sprinkle the chops with the salt and sage. Brown the chops on a microwave browning grill or on top of the stove in a skillet. Place the browned chops in a 13 × 9 in. (33 × 23 cm) microwave or glass baking dish. Peel and slice the apples. Place on top of the chops. Sprinkle with the raisins and maple syrup. Combine the water, flour, and vinegar in a bowl; then stir to completely blend and dissolve the flour. Pour over the chop mixture. Cover tightly with plastic wrap. With the microwave on MEDIUM, cook for 15 to 20 minutes or until the chops are fork-tender; rotate the dish a quarter turn every 5 minutes. Allow to rest 5 minutes before serving.

Yield: 6 servings
Exchange, 1 serving: 2½ high-fat meat, 1 fruit
Calories, 1 serving: 311
Carbohydrates, 1 serving: 18

Apricot-Glazed Ham

| 1 lb. | cooked boneless ham | 500 g |
| 2 T. | dietetic apricot preserves | 30 mL |

Place the ham fat side down on a roasting rack or 8 x 8 in. baking dish. Cover with plastic wrap. With the microwave on MEDIUM, cook for 5 minutes. Turn the ham over. Score the ham with 1 in. (2.5 cm) diamond cuts. Spread 1 T. (15 mL) of the preserves over the ham surface. With the microwave on MEDIUM, cook for 10 minutes. Remove from the microwave and spread the remaining preserves over the surface. Re-cover with new plastic wrap and allow to set for 3 to 5 minutes before slicing.

Yield: 8 servings
Exchange, 1 serving: 1⅔ high-fat meat
Calories, 1 serving: 163
Carbohydrates, 1 serving: negligible

Barbecue-Flavored Pork Loin

| ¾ lb. (4 portions) | tenderized boneless pork loin | 375 g (4 portions) |
| 2 T. | barbecue seasoning and coating mix for chicken | 30 mL |

Place the four portions of tenderized pork loin on a piece of wax paper. Sprinkle 1 T. (15 mL) of the barbecue seasoning on one side of the four loin portions; then press the seasoning into the loin portions with the back of a spoon. Turn the loin portions over and sprinkle the other side with the remaining 1 T. (15 mL) of barbecue seasoning, pressing it in the same way. Coat a 10 in. (25 cm) shallow microwave dish or glass pie pan with vegetable-oil spray. Arrange the loin portions in a single layer on the bottom of the dish. Cover with wax paper. With the microwave on HIGH, cook for 4 minutes, rotating the dish a quarter turn after 2 minutes. Turn the loin portions over and continue cooking on MEDIUM for 2 minutes. Allow to rest 1 minute before serving.

Yield: 4 servings
Exchange, 1 serving: 2 medium-fat meat
Calories, 1 serving: 165
Carbohydrates, 1 serving: 1

Pork Loin with Picante Sauce

1 lb.	split pork loin rib	500 g
2 to 3 T.	water	30 to 45 mL
¼ c.	Pace medium picante sauce	60 mL

Place the pork loin rib in an 8 in. (20 cm) pie plate. Add the water and cover with two layers of paper towels. With the microwave on HIGH, cook for 5 minutes. Turn the meat over, cover with paper towels, and continue cooking on HIGH for an additional 5 minutes. Remove the paper towels, and drain any excess liquid from the bottom of the plate. Cover the meat with the picante sauce. Return to the microwave, uncovered, and cook on MEDIUM for 5 minutes. Allow to set for 3 minutes before serving.

Yield: 8 servings
Exchange, 1 serving: 1⅓ medium-fat meat
Calories, 1 serving: 112
Carbohydrates, 1 serving: 2

Pork Roast with Cherry Sauce

3 lb.	pork loin center rib roast	1½ kg
½ c.	dietetic cherry preserves	125 mL
2 T.	water	30 mL
1 T.	white vinegar	15mL
⅛ t.	salt	½ mL
⅛ t.	nutmeg	½ mL
⅛ t.	cinnamon	½ mL
dash	black pepper	dash

Place the roast, fat side down, on a microwave roasting rack in a large glass or microwave dish. With the microwave on HIGH, cook for 25 minutes. Turn the roast over and continue cooking on MEDIUM for 25 more minutes. Cover the roast with wax paper and set aside. Combine the remaining ingredients in a 1 qt. (1 L) measuring cup. With the microwave on MEDIUM, cook for 3 minutes or until hot. Slice the pork roast almost down to the bone between the ribs. Place the roast on a serving platter. Pour the hot cherry sauce over the top of the roast.

Yield: 20 servings
Exchange, 1 serving: 1½ high-fat meat
Calories, 1 serving: 142
Carbohydrates, 1 serving: negligible

Fin Ribs

3½ lbs.	pork fin ribs	1¾ kg
	salt and pepper to taste	

Cut off as much excess fat as possible. Place the rib pieces in a vegeta-ble-oil-sprayed 3 qt. (3 L) casserole dish. Cover with warm water. Allow to stand for several minutes; then drain thoroughly. Place a lid on the casserole dish or cover securely with plastic wrap. With the microwave on HIGH, cook for 10 minutes. Thoroughly drain off any fat and water. Thn turn the meat over in the dish. Cover and cook for for 10 minutes with the microwave on HIGH. Drain thoroughly. Separate the rib pieces and place the less-done pieces on top. Add salt and pepper to taste. Cover and cook on HIGH in the microwave for 7 to 10 more minutes.

Yield: 20 servings
Exchange, 1 serving: 1¼ high-fat meat
Calories, 1 serving: 130
Carbohydrates, 1 serving: negligible

Pork Cutlets with Oriental Vegetables

1 T.	reduced-calorie margarine	15 mL
1 lb.	pork cutlets	500 g
¼ c.	water	60 mL
¼ lb.	snow peas	250 g
½ c.	sliced green onions	125 mL
½ c.	sliced mushrooms	125 mL
16 oz. bag	frozen Oriental vegetables, partially thawed	454 g bag
2 c.	cold water	500 mL
2½ T.	cornstarch	37 mL
2 T.	soy sauce	30 mL
1 t.	Worcestershire sauce	4 mL
½ t.	browning and seasoning sauce	2 mL
⅛ t.	salt	½ mL

Melt the margarine in a skillet on top of the stove. Cut the pork cutlets into ½ in. (1.25 cm) strips. Quickly brown the cutlets. Place the cutlets in a 3 qt. (3 L) microwave casserole or baking dish. Add the ¼ c. (60 mL) of water to the skillet. Remove any residue that has stuck to the skillet and pour it over the cutlets. Cover with a lid or plastic wrap.

With the microwave on HIGH, cook for 5 minutes. Add the snow peas, green onions, mushrooms, and partially thawed Oriental vegetables. Stir to mix. Cover and cook in the microwave on HIGH for 5 minutes, stirring and turning after 3 minutes. Allow the mixture to rest for 3 minutes.

For crisp vegetables: Remove the meat and vegetables from the dish. Keep hot. Combine 2 c. (500 mL) of cold water and the cornstarch in a measuring cup or bowl. Blend thoroughly to dissolve the cornstarch. Add the soy sauce, Worcestershire sauce, browning sauce, and salt. Return to the microwave, uncovered, and cook on HIGH for 10 to 15 minutes; stir after 2½ minutes, then every 2 minutes until the mixture is thickened and clear. Now, return the meat and vegetables to the dish. Cover and cook on HIGH in the microwave for 2 minutes.

For fully-cooked vegetables: Follow the directions above, but do not remove the vegetables from the dish.

Yield: 8 servings
Exchange, 1 serving: 1 high-fat meat, 2 vegetable
Calories, 1 serving: 159
Carbohydrates, 1 serving: 11

Pork Chop and Sweet Potato Dinner

1 lb. (4 chops)	center-cut pork chops	500 g (4 chops)
¼ t.	thyme	1 mL
¼ t.	marjoram	1 mL
	salt and pepper	
4	sweet potatoes, peeled and sliced	4
1	white onion, thinly sliced	1
18 oz. can	whole tomatoes, with juice	478 g can

Season the pork chops with the thyme, marjoram, salt, and pepper. Place the chops in a microwave casserole or 3 qt. (3 L) baking dish with a lid. Top with the sliced sweet potatoes, onion, and tomatoes with juice. Cover with the lid or plastic wrap. With the microwave on MEDIUM, cook for 25 minutes or until the chops are tender; rotate the dish a quarter turn every 5 minutes.

Yield: 4 servings
Exchange, 1 serving: ½ high-fat meat, 1 bread, 1 vegetable
Calories, 1 serving: 353
Carbohydrates, 1 serving: 21

Pork Steak Teriyaki

1 lb. (4 steaks)	boneless pork shoulder steaks	500 g (4 steaks)
½ c.	teriyaki sauce	125 mL
1 clove	garlic, minced	1 clove

Remove any excess fat from the steaks. Place the steaks in a bowl or marinade container. Add the teriyaki sauce and minced garlic. Cover and allow to marinate for 1 hour or longer. If needed, turn the steaks several times to make sure that the teriyaki sauce is covering them completely. Place the steaks in a single layer on a microwave platter, and cover with plastic wrap. With the microwave on MEDIUM, cook for 3 minutes. Turn the steaks over and re-cover. Continue cooking for 3 more minutes, rotating the platter twice.

Yield: 4 servings
Exchange, 1 serving: 2½ medium-fat meat
Calories, 1 serving: 187
Carbohydrates, 1 serving: negligible

Pork Butt with Cranberries

2 lb.	Boston pork butt	1 kg
¼ c.	water	60 mL
	black pepper, to taste	
1 c.	Tart Cranberry Sauce (page 134)	250 mL

Place the pork butt in a microwave casserole or glass baking dish with a lid. Add the water, then pepper to taste. Cover with the lid or plastic wrap. With the microwave on HIGH, cook for 5 minutes. Turn the roast over, re-cover, and continue cooking on HIGH for 5 minutes. Reduce the heat to MEDIUM, and cook for 10 more minutes; rotate the dish a quarter turn twice during cooking. Remove the roast from the microwave, and drain any excess liquid. Then pour the cranberry sauce over the top of the roast. Cover and return to the microwave. Cook on MEDIUM for 5 minutes, rotating the dish a quarter turn once. Allow the roast to rest for 3 to 4 minutes before serving.

Yield: 10 servings
Exchange, 1 serving: 2½ medium-fat meat, ¼ fruit
Calories, 1 serving: 190
Carbohydrates, 1 serving: 4

Spiced Spareribs

2 lbs.	spareribs	1 kg
2 c.	hot water	500 mL
1½ T.	instant beef broth mix	21 mL
1 t.	allspice	5 mL
¼ t.	black pepper	1 mL

Cut or have the butcher cut the spareribs into six equal portions. Remove any excess fat and discard. Place the spareribs in a single layer in a large microwave or glass dish. Combine the water, broth mix, and spices. Stir to dissolve the broth mix. Pour 1 c. (250 mL) of the bouillon over the spareribs. Cover with plastic wrap. With the microwave on HIGH, cook for 3 minutes or just until boiling. Reduce the heat and continue cooking on MEDIUM for 40 minutes or until fork-tender. Rotate the dish a quarter turn every 8 to 10 minutes, and add extra bouillon as needed. Before serving, allow the spareribs to rest 5 minutes and drain any excess liquid.

Yield: 6 servings
Exchange, 1 serving: 3 high-fat meat
Calories, 1 serving: 285
Carbohydrates, 1 serving: negligible

Spicy Sausage Balls

2 lbs.	seasoned pork sausage	1 kg
5 oz. can	water chestnuts	132 g can

Place the sausage in a mixing bowl. Drain and chop the water chestnuts. Add to meat and mix thoroughly. Form into 20 balls. Place the balls around the edge (with two in the middle) of a 10 in. pie plate. Cover lightly with wax paper or paper towels. Cook on MEDIUM for 4 to 5 minutes, turning the dish one-half rotation every 2 minutes (or using a food rotator). Keep warm until serving time.

Yield: 20 servings
Exchange, 1 serving: 1 high-fat meat
Calories, 1 serving: 96
Carbohydrates, 1 serving: 1

Roast Pork with Onions

3 lbs.	pork loin roast	1½ kg
	salt	
8	onions	8
1 t.	sage	5 mL

Place the pork roast in a microwave baking pan and sprinkle with salt. Cover lightly with three layers of paper towels. With the microwave on HIGH, cook for 10 minutes. Turn the roast over, re-cover, and continue cooking on HIGH for 5 minutes. Drain any excess liquid. Cover with plastic wrap. With the microwave on MEDIUM, cook for 25 minutes. Peel the onions and cut them into eighths. Sprinkle the onions with sage. Lay the onion chunks around the roast in the pan drippings. Re-cover with plastic wrap. With the microwave on MEDIUM, cook for 6 to 7 minutes or until the onions are tender; during cooking, rotate the dish a quarter turn and stir or turn over the onions twice.

Yield: 15 servings
Exchange, 1 serving: 2 high-fat meat, ½ vegetable
Calories, 1 serving: 203
Carbohydrates, 1 serving: 2

Stuffed Picnic Shoulder

2 lb.	boneless fresh picnic shoulder roast	1 kg
	salt and pepper	
16 oz. can	sauerkraut, drained	485 g can
½ t.	rosemary	2 mL

Sprinkle the roast's inside pocket with salt and pepper, and then fill it with the drained sauerkraut. Sprinkle the outside of the roast with salt and rosemary. Roll the roast tightly in plastic wrap. Place the plastic-wrapped roast in a baking dish. With the microwave on MEDIUM, cook for 50 minutes, rotating the dish a quarter turn every 5 minutes. Allow the roast to rest for 10 minutes before removing the plastic wrap. With a sharp knife or fork, prick the surface of the plastic wrap to allow the steam to escape; then *carefully* remove the plastic wrap.

Yield: 10 servings
Exchange, 1 serving: 2 high-fat meat, ½ vegetable
Calories, 1 serving: 199
Carbohydrates, 1 serving: 2

Italian Pork Chops

1 lb. (4 chops)	end-cut pork chops	500 g (4 chops)
1 t.	sage	5 mL
½ t.	rosemary	2 mL
½ t.	oregano	2 mL
½ t.	garlic salt	2 mL
¼ t.	black pepper	1 mL
¼ c.	dry white wine	60 mL

Remove any excess fat from the chops. Wash both sides of the chops, and pat them dry. Combine the herbs in a small bowl. Rub both sides of the chops with the herbs. Place the chops on a microwave platter, and cover with wax paper. With the microwave on HIGH, cook for 5 minutes, rotating the platter once. Drain any liquid. Pour the wine over the chops. Cover with plastic wrap. With the microwave on HIGH, cook for 5 minutes. Allow the chops to rest for 3 to 4 minutes before serving.

Yield: 4 servings
Exchange, 1 serving: 2¼ medium-fat meat
Calories, 1 serving: 179
Carbohydrates, 1 serving: 2

Tasty Pork Tenderloin

1 lb.	boneless pork tenderloin	500 g
1	onion, chopped	1
1 t.	Worcestershire sauce	5 mL
½ t.	chili powder	2 mL
1 c.	chopped tomatoes	250 mL
	salt and pepper	

Cut or have the butcher cut the pork tenderloin into eight thin slices. Place the tenderloin slices in the bottom of a microwave baking dish. Top with the remaining ingredients. Cover with plastic wrap. With the microwave on HIGH, cook for 10 to 12 minutes or until the pork is fork-tender and the onions are cooked.

Yield: 8 servings
Exchange, 1 serving: 1¼ medium-fat meat, ¼ vegetable
Calories, 1 serving: 113
Carbohydrates, 1 serving: 2

Lamb & Veal

Roast Leg of Lamb

4 lb.	leg of lamb roast	2 kg
1 clove	garlic	1 clove
1 t.	ginger	5 mL
	salt and pepper	

Wipe the meat with a damp cloth. Make four gashes in the roast using a sharp knife. Cut the garlic into four slivers and insert one sliver into each gash. Rub the meat with the ginger. Add salt and pepper as desired. Place the roast, fat side down, on a microwave rack in a 13 x 9 in. (33 . 23 cm) microwave baking dish. With the microwave on MEDIUM, cook for 25 minutes. Turn the lamb over and continue cooking on MEDIUM for 25 minutes. Cover with aluminum foil and allow the roast to rest for 10 minutes before serving.

Yield: 10 servings
Exchange, 1 serving: 3 high-fat meat
Calories, 1 serving: 310
Carbohydrates, 1 serving: 2

Lamb and Prunes

1 medium	onion, chopped	1 medium
1 t.	water	5 mL
1 T.	tomato paste	15 mL
¼ c.	water	60 mL
2½ lbs.	lean lamb shoulder chops	1 kg

1½ c.	pitted prunes	375 mL
½ t.	cinnamon	2 mL
¼ t.	nutmeg	2 mL
	juice of 1 lemon	

Combine the onion and 1 t. (5 mL) of water in a 2½ or 3 qt. (2.5 or 3 L) baking dish. Cover with plastic wrap, and cook on HIGH, in the microwave for 1 minute. Stir in the tomato paste and ¼ c. (60 mL) water. Place the lamb chops in the dish. With the microwave on MEDIUM, cook for 12 minutes, turning the dish at least once. Turn the chops over. Place the prunes around the chops and add the remaining ingredients. With the microwave on MEDIUM, cook 8 or 10 minutes more or until the chops are fork-tender.

Yield: 8 servings
Exchange, 1 serving: 3 high-fat meat, ½ fruit
Calories, 1 serving: 388
Carbohydrates, 1 serving: 2

Lamb Kabobs

2 lb.	lean lamb steak, ¾ in. (18 mm) thick	1 kg
⅓ c.	lemon juice	90 mL
2. T.	sunflower oil	30 mL
1	onion, minced	1
1 t.	salt	5 mL
½ lb.	mushroom caps, cleaned	250 g

Cut the lamb steak into 1 in. (2.5 cm) squares. Combine the lemon juice, oil, onion, and salt in a bowl or marinade dish. Add the lamb squares and marinate 2 hours or longer. Drain the marinade from the lamb. Arrange the lamb alternately with the mushroom caps on a skewer. Arrange the kabobs in an 8 in. (20 cm)-square microwave dish. Cover with wax paper. With the microwave on MEDIUM, cook for 10 to 12 minutes or until the meat is done. During cooking, turn and rearrange the skewers and brush with marinade twice.

Yield: 8 servings
Exchange, 1 serving: 3 high-fat meat, ¼ vegetable
Calories, 1 serving: 310
Carbohydrates, 1 serving: 2

Lamb and Cheese with Vegetables

2½ lbs.	lamb cubes	1 kg
6 cubes (in.)	feta cheese	6 cubes (2.5 cm)
6 cubes (in.)	kefalotire cheese	6 cubes (2.5 cm)
6 small	carrots, quartered	6 small
6 stalks	celery, quartered	6 stalks
6 medium	potatoes, quartered	6 medium
6 medium	onions, quartered	6 medium
	juice of 1 lemon	
	salt and pepper	

Spray a 12 × 9 in. (33 × 23 cm) baking dish with vegetable-oil spray. Layer the ingredients in the order given. Cover with plastic wrap. With the microwave on MEDIUM, cook for 15 to 17 minutes or until the meat is fork-tender.

Yield: 12 servings
Exchange, 1 serving: 3½ high-fat meat, ½ bread
Calories, 1 serving: 415
Carbohydrates, 1 serving: 9

Barbecued Lamb

4 lb.	leg of lamb roast	2 kg
1 t.	Dijon mustard	5 mL
1 t.	ginger	5 mL
½ t.	salt	2 mL
¼ t.	pepper	1 mL
2	onions, sliced	2
1 c.	hot water	250 mL
2 T.	bottled chili sauce	30 mL
1 T.	Worcestershire sauce	15 mL
1 T.	white vinegar	15 mL

Wipe the meat with a damp cloth. Combine the mustard, ginger, salt, and pepper in a small bowl. Rub the meat with this mustard-ginger mixture. Place the roast, fat side down, on a microwave rack in a 13 × 9 in. (33 × 23 cm) microwave baking dish. Cover the roast with the onion slices. With the microwave on MEDIUM, cook for 25 minutes. Combine the remaining ingredients in a bowl. Stir to blend. Turn the lamb over and baste it with the chili sauce mixture. Return the roast to the microwave and continue cooking on MEDIUM for 25 minutes. Baste the roast every 5 minutes with the chili mixture. Cover the roast with aluminum foil, and allow it to rest for 10 minutes before serving.

Yield: 10 servings
Exchange, 1 serving: 3 high-fat meat
Calories, 1 serving: 316
Carbohydrates, 1 serving: 2

Lamb Stew

2 c.	water	500mL
2 T.	all-purpose flour	30 mL
2 lb.	lean lamb cubes	1 kg
5	carrots, cut in cubes	5
4	potatoes, cut in cubes	4
3	onions, cut in eighths	3
3	turnips, cut in cubes	3
3	tomatoes, cut in eighths	3
	salt and pepper	

Combine the water and flour in a 4 qt. (4 L) microwave casserole or baking dish. Stir to completely blend and dissolve the flour. Add the remaining ingredients. Cover with a lid or plastic wrap. With the microwave on MEDIUM, cook for 45 to 50 minutes; rotate the dish after 10 minutes, then every 5 minutes.

Yield: 10 servings
Exchange, 1 serving: 2 high-fat meat, ½ bread, ¼ vegetable
Calories, 1 serving: 298
Carbohydrates, 1 serving: 8

Lamb and Rice au Gratin

2 c.	diced cooked lamb	500 mL
2 c.	cooked rice	500 mL
10 oz. can	cream of celery soup	300 g can
4 oz. can	mushroom stems and pieces, drained	120 g can
½ c.	skim milk	125 mL
1 t.	rosemary	5 mL
	salt and pepper	
½ c.	shredded sharp Cheddar cheese	125 mL

Combine the ingredients, except the Cheddar cheese, in a large mixing bowl. Stir to thoroughly mix. Pour this mixture into a 2 qt. (2 L) microwave casserole or baking dish. Cover with a lid or plastic wrap. With the microwave on HIGH, cook for 5 minutes. Stir the mixture; then cover and continue cooking on MEDIUM for 5 minutes. Sprinkle with cheese. Return the mixture, uncovered, to the microwave, and cook on MEDIUM for 10 minutes or until the mixture is hot and the cheese is melted.

Yield: 10 servings
Exchange, 1 serving: 2 high-fat meat, 1 bread
Calories, 1 serving: 281
Carbohydrates, 1 serving: 16

Shepherd's Pie

1½ c.	cold water	375 mL
1½ T.	all-purpose flour	21 mL
1½ T.	instant chicken broth mix	21 mL
3 c.	mashed potatoes, from instant	750 mL
2 c.	diced cooked lamb	500 mL

Combine the water and flour in a 2 c. (500 mL) measuring cup. Stir to completely blend and dissolve the flour. With the microwave on HIGH, cook for 2 minutes. Stir and add the chicken broth mix. Stir to blend. Return to the microwave and continue cooking for 1 to 2 minutes or until the mixture is thickened; stir twice during cooking. Place half of the potatoes on the bottom of a 2 qt. (2 L) greased microwave casserole or baking dish. Arrange the cooked lamb and gravy over the top of the potatoes. Cover with the remaining potatoes. With the microwave on MEDIUM, cook, uncovered, for 15 to 17 minutes or until the pie is hot—rotating the dish after 3 minutes and then every 2 minutes.

Yield: 8 servings
Exchange, 1 serving: 1 high-fat meat, ⅔ bread
Calories, 1 serving: 117
Carbohydrates, 1 serving: 11

Breaded Veal Cutlets

1½ lb. (6 cutlets)	veal cutlets	750 g (6 cutlets)
	salt and pepper	
1 c.	fine dry bread crumbs	250 mL
1 T.	paprika	15 mL
2	egg whites, slightly beaten	2
2 t.	browning and seasoning sauce	10 mL

Season the cutlets with salt and pepper. Combine the bread crumbs and paprika in a flat dish, stirring to mix. Combine the egg whites and browning sauce in flat dish, stirring to blend. Dip the cutlets into the bread crumbs, into the egg mixture, and again into the bread crumbs. Place the cutlets on a roasting rack in a shallow microwave baking dish. With the microwave on HIGH, cook for 5 minutes. Turn the cutlets over. Return to the microwave and continue cooking on MEDIUM for 10 minutes or until the meat is fork-tender. Cover with aluminum foil or keep hot in a warm oven for 5 minutes before serving.

Yield: 6 servings
Exchange, 1 serving: 2 medium-fat meat, ⅔ bread
Calories, 1 serving: 210
Carbohydrates, 1 serving: 11

Veal Rump Roast

3 lb.	veal rump roast	1½ kg
10 oz. can	beef vegetable soup	280 g can
2	bay leaves	2
1 sprig	parsley, chopped	1 sprig
1 t.	salt	5 mL
¼ t.	pepper	1 mL
2 T.	all-purpose flour	30 mL

Place the roast, fat side down, in a 3 qt. (3 L) microwave casserole or baking dish. Cover with a lid or plastic wrap. With the microwave on MEDIUM, cook for 30 minutes. Remove the roast from the dish; then drain the juice into a measuring cup. Return the roast to the dish, fat side up. Pour the beef vegetable soup over the roast. Add the bay leaves, parsley, salt, and pepper. Re-cover and continue cooking on LOW for 30 to 35 minutes or until the roast is fork-tender. Remove the roast to the serving platter and keep hot. Combine the flour with the roast drippings in a measuring cup. Beat to blend thoroughly. Pour and stir the flour mixture into the soup mixture in the dish. Return to the microwave, and cook on HIGH for 1 to 2 minutes or until thickened; stir after the first minute and then every 30 seconds.

Yield: 10 servings
Exchange, 1 serving: 2½ lean meat, ¼ bread
Calories, 1 serving: 162
Carbohydrates, 1 serving: 3

Mock Chicken

2 lbs.	boneless lean veal round steak	1 kg
	salt and pepper	
1	green pepper, chopped	1
½ c.	chopped celery	125 mL
⅓ c.	water	90 mL
1 t.	Worcestershire sauce	5 mL
½ c.	sliced mushrooms	125 mL

Cut the veal steak into eight serving pieces. Salt and pepper each piece. Place in a 2 qt. (2 L) microwave casserole or baking dish. Add the green pepper, celery, water, and Worcestershire sauce. Stir to mix slightly. Cover with a lid or plastic wrap. With the microwave on HIGH, cook for

2 minutes. Reduce the heat and cook on MEDIUM for 10 minutes, turning the dish once. Rearrange the meat, add the mushrooms, cover, and then return to the microwave. Continue cooking on MEDIUM for 10 minutes or until the meat is fork-tender.

Yield: 8 servings
Exchange, 1 serving: 3 lean meat
Calories, 1 serving: 159
Carbohydrates, 1 serving: negligible

Veal Parmigiana

1 lb.	lean veal steak, sliced very thin	500 g
¼ c.	fine dry bread crumbs	60 mL
¼ c.	grated Parmesan cheese	60 mL
1 t.	salt	5 mL
¼ t.	pepper	1 mL
1	egg, beaten	1
18 oz. can	tomatoes	514 g can
8 oz. can	tomato sauce	240 g can
1	onion, minced	1
2 cloves	garlic, minced	2 cloves
dash	oregano	dash
3 oz.	mozzarella cheese, shredded	90 g

Cut the veal into serving-size pieces. Mix the bread crumbs, Parmesan cheese, salt, and pepper. Dip both sides of the veal into the egg; then coat them lightly with the crumb mixture. Place the breaded veal in a 3 qt. (3 L) microwave casserole or baking dish. Combine the tomatoes, tomato sauce, onion, garlic, and oregano in a bowl. Stir to blend. Pour the tomato mixture over the veal. Cover with a lid or plastic wrap. With the microwave on MEDIUM, cook for 15 minutes, rotating the dish a quarter turn after 7 minutes. Carefully remove the plastic wrap. Top with the shredded mozzarella. Now, return to the microwave and continue cooking on MEDIUM for 6 to 7 minutes. Allow to rest for 3 to 4 minutes before serving.

Yield: 10 servings
Exchange, 1 serving: 1 high-fat meat, 1 vegetable
Calories, 1 serving: 137
Carbohydrates, 1 serving: 8

Chicken

Chicken in Sweet Wine Sauce

3 lb.	frying chicken	1½ kg
1 clove	garlic, minced	1 clove
1 t.	oregano	5 mL
3	peppercorns	3
1 t.	salt	5 mL
5	potatoes	5
¾ c.	water	190 mL
3	onions, sliced	3
10	pitted prunes	10
2 T.	raisins	30 mL
3	bay leaves	3
1 c.	muscatel wine	250 mL
2 T.	liquid sugar replacement	30 mL

Wash and dry the chicken. Mash together the garlic, oregano, pepper-corns, and salt. Rub both the inside and outside of the chicken with this mixture. Place the chicken in a 4 qt. (4 L) microwave casserole or baking dish. Peel the potatoes and cut them into chunks. Add the potatoes, water, onions, prunes, raisins, and bay leaves to the chicken. Cover with a lid or plastic wrap. With the microwave on HIGH, cook for 25 minutes or until the chicken is fork-tender; rotate the dish a quarter turn every 5 minutes. Blend the wine and liquid sugar replacement in a cup; then pour it over the chicken. Return to the microwave, uncov-ered, and cook on MEDIUM for 5 minutes or just until boiling. Remove from the microwave, re-cover, and allow to rest for 8 to 10 minutes before serving.

Yield: 10 servings
Exchange, 1 serving: 1 medium-fat meat, ½ bread
Calories, 1 serving: 132
Carbohydrates, 1 serving: 8

Chicken Fricassee

3 lb.	frying chicken, cut up	1½ kg
1 c.	water	250 mL
½ t.	salt	2 mL
1	onion, chopped	1
2 stalks	celery, with leaves	2
2 sprigs	parsley, chopped	2 sprigs
1	bay leaf	1
2 T.	instant chicken broth mix	30 mL
	water	
½ c.	skim milk	125 mL
½ c.	all-purpose flour	125 mL

Wash the chicken, and then pat it dry and remove the skin. If desired, the chicken may be cut into smaller pieces. Place the chicken pieces in a 4 qt. (4 L) microwave casserole or baking dish. Add the 1 cup. (250 mL) water and salt. Cover with a lid or plastic wrap. With the microwave on HIGH, cook for 10 minutes, rotating the dish after 5 minutes. Rearrange the chicken. Add the onion, celery, parsley, and bay leaf. Re-cover and continue cooking on MEDIUM for 20 minutes or until the chicken is tender. Move the chicken to a platter. Remove the meat from the bones, if desired. Skim any excess fat from the liquid. Pour the liquid into a 1 qt. (1 L) measuring cup. Stir in the chicken broth mix and add enough water to make 3 cups (750 mL). Pour this broth mixture back into the casserole. Combine the milk and flour, stirring to blend completely. Slowly add this flour-milk mixture to the broth. Stir to thoroughly mix. Cook, uncovered, with the microwave on HIGH for 5 minutes; stir vigorously after 2 minutes, and then every 30 seconds. Stir and allow to rest until thickened. If the mixture does not thicken to desired consistency, return to the microwave for 2 minutes, stirring every 30 seconds. Now, add the chicken, cover, and return to the microwave. Cook on MEDIUM for 2 minutes.

Yield: 10 servings
Exchange, 1 serving: 1 medium-fat meat, ⅓ bread
Calories, 1 serving: 101
Carbohydrates, 1 serving: 5

Chicken Breast with Mushroom Sauce

8 oz.	frozen chicken breast, stuffed with shrimp, cod and crabmeat	240 g
½ c.	canned cream of mushroom soup, undiluted	125 mL
1 T.	water	15 mL

Slightly thaw the chicken breast, and pull off the skin. Remove the chicken breast from its metal container, and secure the stuffing with toothpicks. Place the stuffing side up in an 8 in. (20 cm) shallow microwave dish or glass pie pan. Combine the soup and water in a cup, mixing to blend. Spread the soup mixture over the chicken breast. Cover with plastic wrap. With the microwave on HIGH, cook for 4 minutes, rotating the dish once. Allow the chicken to rest for 3 to 4 minutes before serving.

Yield: 2 servings
Exchange, 1 serving: 2 lean meat, ⅓ bread
Calories, 1 serving: 143
Carbohydrates, 1 serving: 4

Roast Chicken and Dressing

3 lb.	frying chicken	1½ kg
4 c.	dry bread cubes	1000 mL
½ c.	sliced green onions	125 mL
2 t.	sage	10 mL
½ c.	boiling water	125 mL
½ c.	orange juice	125 mL
	salt and pepper	
2 T.	browning and seasoning sauce	30 mL
1 t.	Worcestershire sauce	5 mL

Wash the chicken and cut off any excess fat. Discard the neck and organs. Salt the cavity of the chicken. Combine the bread cubes, green onions, and sage in a large bowl. Add the boiling water and orange juice to this bread mixture. Stir to mix. Allow to stand until the liquid has been absorbed by the bread. Season with salt and pepper. Press this dressing tightly into the cavity of the chicken; then press any remaining dressing into the neck area. Tie or secure the dressing, legs, and wings of the chicken with toothpicks. Place the chicken, breast side down, onto a roasting rack in a shallow microwave baking dish. Combine the browning sauce and Worcestershire sauce in a small bowl; then brush it lightly over the bottom of the chicken. With the microwave on HIGH, cook for 18 minutes. Drain any excess grease from the bottom of the dish. Turn the chicken over, breast side up. Brush with the browning sauce mixture; then rotate the dish to make sure you are completely covering the chicken with the browning sauce mixture. Return to the microwave and continue cooking on MEDIUM for 10 minutes. Brush the browning sauce mixture over the chicken. Rotate the dish one-half turn and continue cooking on MEDIUM for 10 minutes. Remove the chicken from the microwave. Cover the chicken with aluminum foil or keep it hot in a warm oven for 5 to 10 minutes before serving.

Yield: 10 servings
Exchange, 1 serving: 1 medium-fat meat, 2 bread
Calories, 1 serving: 230
Carbohydrates, 1 serving: 29

Old-Fashioned Chicken Dinner

3 lb.	frying chicken, cut up	1½ kg
1 t.	salt	5 mL
2 c.	water	500 mL
4	potatoes, peeled and cut in pieces	4
6	onions, quartered	6
1 small	cauliflower, cleaned and cut in pieces	1 small
6	carrots, cleaned and cut in half	6
¼ head	cabbage	¼ head

Wash the chicken and remove any excess fat. Place the chicken in a 4 qt. (4 L) or larger microwave casserole or baking dish. Sprinkle with salt and add water. Cover with a lid or plastic wrap. With the microwave on HIGH, cook for 10 minutes. Rearrange the chicken. Add the vegetables; then re-cover and continue cooking on HIGH for 10 minutes. Reduce the heat to MEDIUM and continue cooking for 10 to 15 minutes or until the vegetables are tender; rotate the dish a quarter turn every 5 minutes.

Yield: 10 servings
Exchange, 1 serving: 1 medium-fat meat, ½ bread, ½ vegetable
Calories, 1 serving: 128
Carbohydrates, 1 serving: 10

Chicken Cacciatore

3 lb.	frying chicken, cut up	1½ kg
15 oz. can	tomato sauce	450 g can
6 oz. can	tomato paste	180 g can
1 c.	water	250 mL
½ c.	dry red wine	125 mL
¾ c.	chopped onions	190 mL
½ c.	sliced mushrooms	125 mL
2 cloves	garlic, minced	2 cloves
1 t.	oregano	5 mL
½ t.	salt	2 mL
¼ t.	thyme	1 mL
¼ t.	basil	1 mL

If desired, wash the chicken and cut it into smaller pieces. Set aside. Combine the remaining ingredients in 4 qt. (4 L) microwave casserole or baking dish. Stir to completely blend. Now, add the chicken pieces. Cover with a lid or plastic wrap. With the microwave on HIGH, cook for 10 minutes. Rearrange the chicken pieces. Continue cooking on HIGH for 15 minutes, rotating the dish a quarter turn every 5 minutes.

Yield: 10 servings
Exchange, 1 serving: 1 medium-fat meat, 1 vegetable, ⅓ bread
Calories, 1 serving: 139
Carbohydrates, 1 serving: 11

Lemon Chicken

3 lb.	frying chicken, cut up	1½ kg
3 T.	butter	45 mL
1 clove	garlic, sliced	1 clove
1 t.	salt	5 mL
dash	black pepper	dash
½ c.	lemon juice	125 mL
¼ c.	water	60 mL
2 t.	paprika	10 mL

Wash the chicken and remove any excess fat and skin. Pat the chicken dry and then set it aside. Combine the butter, garlic, salt, and pepper in a 4 qt. (4 L) microwave casserole or baking dish. Cook, covered, with the microwave on HIGH for 1 minute or until the butter is melted. Stir the lemon juice and water into the butter mixture. Place a roast rack inside of the casserole dish. Sprinkle the chicken pieces lightly with paprika and then arrange them on top of the rack. Cover with a lid or plastic wrap. With the microwave on MEDIUM, cook for 35 to 40 minutes or until the chicken is fork-tender; rotate the dish twice during cooking and add extra water if needed.

Yield: 10 servings
Exchange, 1 serving: 1 medium-fat meat
Calories, 1 serving: 81
Carbohydrates, 1 serving: negligible

Chicken with Cherries

3 lb.	frying chicken, cut up	1½ kg
1 c.	hot water	250 mL
1 T.	instant chicken broth mix	15 mL
2 T.	all-purpose flour	30 mL
1 c.	cold water	250 mL
¼ t.	cinnamon	1 mL
⅛ t.	allspice	½ mL
⅛ t.	red food coloring	½ mL
2 c.	Bing or dark cherries, pitted	500 mL

Wash the chicken and cut it into small pieces. If desired, brown the chicken on a microwave browning grill or on top of the stove in a skillet. Place the chicken in a 4 qt. (4 L) microwave casserole or glass baking dish. Dissolve the chicken broth mix in the hot water; then pour it over the chicken. Cover with a lid or plastic wrap. With the microwave on HIGH, cook for 10 minutes. Rearrange the chicken pieces. Combine the flour, cold water, cinnamon, allspice, and food coloring in a measuring cup or gravy shaker. Stir or shake to blend thoroughly. Slowly pour this flour mixture over the chicken, stirring to mix thoroughly. Re-cover and cook with the microwave on MEDIUM for 20 minutes. Stir and rotate the dish a quarter turn after the first 5 minutes, then every 3 to 4 minutes. Add the cherries after 15 minutes.

Yield: 10 servings
Exchange, 1 serving: 1 medium-fat meat, ⅓ fruit
Calories, 1 serving: 96
Carbohydrates, 1 serving: 5

Diced Chicken with Almonds

2 c.	diced raw chicken	500 mL
2 T.	soy sauce	30 mL
10 oz. pkg.	frozen green peas, thawed	300 g pkg
1 c.	diced celery	250 mL
½ c.	sliced mushrooms	125 mL
¾ c.	boiling water	190 mL
1 T.	cornstarch	15 mL
¼ c.	cold water	60 mL
⅓ c.	toasted almonds	90 mL

Place the diced chicken in a 2 qt. (2 L) microwave casserole or baking dish. Sprinkle with the soy sauce. Stir to completely coat. Cover with a lid or plastic wrap. With the microwave on HIGH, cook for 2 minutes. Add the peas, celery, mushrooms, and boiling water. Continue cooking on HIGH for 2 minutes. Stir to mix. Combine the cornstarch and ¼ c. (60 mL) cold water in a cup. Stir to completely blend. Slowly pour and stir the cornstarch mixture into the chicken mixture. Re-cover and continue cooking on MEDIUM for 5 to 6 minutes or until the mixture is thickened and clear. Remove from the microwave; then add the almonds.

Yield: 8 servings
Exchange, 1 serving: 1 lean meat, ½ vegetable
Calories, 1 serving: 69
Carbohydrates, 1 serving: 3

Coq au Vin

3 lb.	frying chicken, cut up	1½ kg
10 small	onions, peeled	10 small
10 small	carrots, cleaned	10 small
8 oz. can	mushrooms, with liquid	240 g can
2 T.	chopped parsley	30 mL
2 cloves	garlic, sliced	2 cloves
1	bay leaf	1
¼ t.	savory	1 mL
¼ t.	thyme	1 mL
2 c.	dry red wine	500 mL
2 T.	all-purpose flour	30 mL

If desired, wash the chicken and cut it up into small serving-size pieces. Brown the chicken pieces on a microwave browning grill or on top of the stove in a skillet. Combine the onions, carrots, mushrooms (with liquid), parsley, garlic, bay leaf, savory, and thyme in a 4 qt. (4 L) microwave casserole or baking dish. Now, add the chicken pieces. Cover with a lid or plastic wrap. With the microwave on HIGH, cook for 10 minutes, rotating the dish every 3 to 4 minutes. Rearrange the chicken pieces. Combine the wine and flour in a measuring cup or shaker, and blend thoroughly. Pour this wine mixture over the chicken. Re-cover and cook on MEDIUM in the microwave for 30 to 35 minutes or until the chicken and vegetables are tender.

Yield: 10 servings
Exchange, 1 serving: 1 medium-fat meat, 1 vegetable
Calories, 1 serving: 115
Carbohydrates, 1 serving: 6

Roast Chicken with Applesauce

4 lb.	roasting chicken	2 kg
	salt and pepper	
2	apples	2
1 c.	unsweetened applesauce	250 mL

Wash the chicken and remove any excess fat. Sprinkle both the inside and outside of the chicken with salt and pepper. Peel, core, and quarter one apple. Place the apple quarters inside the body cavity of the chicken. Tie the legs and wings to the chicken body. Place the chicken, breast side down, on a roast rack in a microwave baking dish. Cook, uncovered, in the microwave on HIGH for 15 minutes. Allow the chicken to rest 5 minutes. Meanwhile, peel, core, and thinly slice the second apple. Combine the applesauce and apple slices. Remove the roasting rack and drain any excess grease from the baking dish. Turn the chicken , breast side up, into the baking dish. Spread with the applesauce mixture. Cover with plastic wrap. Continue cooking for 20 minutes on MEDIUM, basting the chicken with the applesauce mixture and rotating the dish a quarter turn every 5 minutes. Allow the chicken to rest 5 minutes before serving.

Yield: 10 servings
Exchange, 1 serving: 1½ medium-fat meat, ¾ fruit
Calories, 1 serving: 155
Carbohydrates, 1 serving: 12

Chicken Jambalaya

1½ c.	cooked chicken	375 mL
1½ c.	cooked tomatoes	375 mL
1 c.	cooked rice	250 mL
1	onion, chopped	1
½	green pepper, chopped	½
½ c.	chopped celery	125 mL
½ t.	salt	2 mL
⅛ t.	black pepper	½ mL

Combine the chicken, tomatoes, and rice in a 3 qt. (3 L) microwave casserole or baking dish. Cover with a lid or plastic wrap. With the microwave on MEDIUM, cook for 5 minutes, rotating the dish every 2 minutes. Add the onion, green pepper, celery, salt, and pepper. Stir to mix. Re-cover and continue cooking on MEDIUM for 15 minutes, rotating the dish every 5 minutes. Allow the Jambalaya to rest 5 minutes before serving.

Yield: 3 servings
Exchange, 1 serving: 2 lean meat, 1 bread, 1 vegetable
Calories, 1 serving: 215
Carbohydrates, 1 serving: 23

Cayenne Chicken

3 lb.	frying chicken, cut up	1½ kg
½ c.	lemon juice	125 mL
2 T.	tomato paste	30 mL
2 cloves	garlic, mashed	2 cloves
2 t.	salt	10 mL
2 t.	cayenne	10 mL
1 t.	paprika	5 mL
½ t.	dry mustard	2 mL
½ c.	safflower oil	125 mL

Wash the chicken and cut it into small pieces. Place the chicken pieces in a marinade or glass bowl. Combine the remaining ingredients, except the safflower oil, in a blender. Blend on LOW speed. With the blender still on LOW, slowly pour the oil into the blender through a feed tube. Blend for 2 more minutes. Pour this mixture over the chicken.

Chill and allow to marinate at least 6 hours or overnight. Remove the chicken from the marinade, reserving the marinade. Place the chicken on a microwave platter or glass plate. Cover with wax paper. With the microwave on HIGH, cook for 5 minutes, rotating the platter a quarter turn after 2 minutes. Turn the chicken over, and baste with the reserve marinade. Then continue cooking on MEDIUM for 10 minutes or until the chicken is fork-tender; rotate the dish a quarter turn and baste every 5 minutes. Allow the chicken to rest 5 minutes before serving.

Yield: 10 servings
Exchange, 1 serving: 1 high-fat meat
Calories, 1 serving: 125
Carbohydrates, 1 serving: negligible

Chicken Breasts

1 (8 oz. each)	chicken breasts	2 (240 g each)
2 T.	butter, melted	30 mL
2 T.	safflower oil	30 mL
1 t.	butter flavoring	5 mL
¼ t.	salt	1 mL
dash	white pepper	dash
	paprika	

Skin the chicken breasts and cut them in half. Combine the butter, oil, butter flavoring, salt, and white pepper in a shallow bowl. Dip each half-breast into this butter mixture. Place on the bottom of a microwave platter or pie pan. Cover with wax paper. With the microwave on HIGH, cook for 5 minutes. Remove the wax paper. Baste with the remaining butter mixture. Sprinkle lightly with paprika. Cook, uncovered, with the microwave on HIGH for 5 more minutes; rotate the dish a quarter turn after 2 minutes. Remove the chicken from the microwave, baste with the remaining butter mixture, and sprinkle lightly with paprika.

Yield: 4 servings
Exchange, 1 serving: 2 lean meat
Calories, 1 serving: 115
Carbohydrates, 1 serving: negligible

Chicken with Rice

Chicken:

3 lb.	frying chicken, cut up	1½ kg
1	onion, sliced	1
2 cloves	garlic, mashed	2 cloves
2	bay leaves	2
2 c.	hot water	500 mL
½ t.	salt	2 mL

Rice:

1 c.	uncooked rice	250 mL
2 c.	hot water	500 mL
1½ T.	instant chicken broth mix	21 mL
½ c.	finely chopped onion	125 mL
½ c.	cooked tomatoes	125 mL
¼ c.	finely sliced green pepper	60 mL
2	pimientos, mashed	2
1 T.	parsley	15 mL

Wash the chicken and cut it into smaller pieces. Place the chicken in a 4 qt. (4 L) microwave casserole or baking dish. Add the onion slices, garlic, bay leaves, water, and salt. Cover with a lid or plastic wrap. With the microwave on HIGH, cook for 5 minutes. Rearrange the chicken; then return to the microwave and cook on HIGH for 5 minutes. Rearrange the chicken again, re-cover, and continue cooking on HIGH for 10 minutes. Remove the chicken. Skim off any excess grease from the broth. Pour the broth into a 1 qt. (1 L) measuring cup. Add enough water to make 2 cups (500 mL); then return this liquid to the casserole. Stir in the remaining ingredients. Place the chicken pieces on top. Cover and cook on MEDIUM in the microwave for 15 minutes, rotating the dish a quarter turn every 5 minutes. Allow the chicken to rest 5 minutes before serving.

Yield: 10 servings
Exchange, 1 serving: 1 medium-fat meat, ⅓ bread
Calories, 1 serving: 100
Carbohydrates, 1 serving: 5

Other Poultry

Quail with Sherry

6	quail	6
2 cloves	garlic, crushed	2 cloves
½ c.	coarsley chopped onion	125 mL
	salt and pepper	
1 T.	browning and seasoning sauce	15 mL
¼ c.	sherry	60 mL
1 small	tart apple, chopped	1 small

Wash and clean the quail. Tie the legs and tail together with a cotton thread. Cover the ends of the wings and legs with aluminum foil. Place the quail, breast side down, on a microwave platter. Cover with the garlic, onion, salt, and pepper. Cover with wax paper. With the microwave on HIGH, cook for 2 minutes. Combine the browning sauce and sherry in a small cup. Turn the quail over. Brush the quail completely with the sherry mixture. Return to the microwave and continue cooking on MEDIUM for 2 minutes. Remove the aluminum foil from the quail, brush with the sherry mixture, and add the chopped apple. Return to the microwave, and cook on MEDIUM for 2 minutes. Brush with the sherry mixture. Cover with aluminum foil and allow to rest 3 to 4 minutes before serving.

Yield: 6 servings
Exchange, 1 serving: 3 medium-fat meat
Calories, 1 serving: 210
Carbohydrates, 1 serving: 2

Marinated Quail

6	quail	6
½ c.	dry white wine	125 mL
2 T.	vegetable oil	30 mL
½ c.	chopped green onion	125 mL
1 clove	garlic, crushed	1 clove
1 t.	parsley	5 mL

Wash the quail and split it down the backbone. Lay it flat in a marinade dish or baking dish. Combine the remaining ingredients, and stir to blend. Pour over the quail. Cover and allow to marinate in the refrigerator for 2 days, turning the quail or brushing it with the marinade. Then remove the quail and place it flat on a microwave platter. (You may have to cook them in the microwave in two batches.) Cover with plastic wrap. With the microwave on HIGH, cook for 3 minutes. Turn the quail over, and brush it with the marinade; then continue cooking for 2 to 3 minutes or until the quail is fork-tender. Keep hot in a warm oven. Allow the quail to rest for 2 to 3 minutes before serving.

Yield: 6 servings
Exchange, 1 serving: 3 medium-fat meat
Calories, 1 serving: 225
Carbohydrates, 1 serving: 3

Cornish Game Hens in Sherry

4	Cornish game hens	4
	salt	
2 T.	reduced-calorie margarine	30 mL
1 c.	sweet sherry	250 mL
¼ c.	all-purpose flour	60 mL
½ c.	chopped onions	125 mL
2 T.	liquid sugar replacement	30 mL
	yellow food coloring	

Wash the hens and remove the giblets. Salt the cavity. Tie the legs and tail together with a cotton thread. Cover the ends of the wings and legs with aluminum foil. Place the hens, breast side down, on a microwave platter. Cover with wax paper. With the microwave on HIGH, cook for 7 minutes. Set aside. Melt the margarine in a 1 qt. (1 L) measuring cup.

Stir in the sherry, flour, onions, sugar replacement, and a drop or two of yellow food coloring. With the microwave on HIGH, cook for 1 minute, and then stir thoroughly. Continue cooking on HIGH for 1 minute or until the mixture is thickened, stirring several times. Remove the foil from the hens and brush the sherry mixture on their bottoms. Then turn them over, breast side up, and brush with the sherry mixture. Cover with wax paper. Return to the microwave, and cook on HIGH for 12 minutes, rotating the dish a quarter turn and basting with the sherry mixture every 3 to 4 minutes. Remove the hens from the microwave, and take off the wax paper. Cover with aluminum foil or keep hot in a warm oven for 15 minutes before serving.

Yield: 4 servings
Exchange, 1 serving: 4 high-fat meat, 1 bread
Calories, 1 serving: 492
Carbohydrates, 1 serving: 15

Turkey Loaf

10 oz. can	turkey noodle soup	280 g can
1 c.	cooked turkey	250 mL
1½ c.	soft bread crumbs	375 mL
2	eggs, slightly beaten	2
3 T.	chopped celery	45 mL
1 T.	chopped parsley	15 mL
1 T.	chopped pimiento	15 mL
½ t.	salt	2 mL

Drain the soup liquid into a large bowl. Combine the turkey and soup solids in a food processor. Process with a steel blade just until the meat is shredded. Add to the soup liquid. Next, add the remaining ingredients and stir to completely blend. Pack into a greased loaf pan. Cover with wax paper. With the microwave on MEDIUM, cook for 25 minutes; rotate the dish a quarter turn after 10 minutes, then every 5 minutes. Allow the loaf to rest for 5 minutes before serving.

Yield: 8 servings
Exchange, 1 serving: 1 lean meat, ⅓ bread, ⅓ fat
Calories, 1 serving: 93
Carbohydrates, 1 serving: 6

Roast Duck

5 lb.	duck	2½ kg
2 cloves	garlic, minced	2 cloves
	salt and pepper	
3 c.	quartered apples	750 mL
1 c.	raisins	250 mL
1 c.	orange juice	250 mL
1 T.	browning and seasoning sauce	15 mL

Wash the duck and trim the fat; discard the giblets. Combine the garlic, salt, and pepper in a small bowl. Rub this garlic mixture over both the entire outside and cavity of the duck. Place the apples and raisins in the cavity. Secure the cavity with toothpicks. Cover the ends of the wings and legs with aluminum foil. Tie the wings and legs to the body with cotton thread. Prick the skin several places with a sharp fork. Place the duck, breast side down, on a roasting rack in a baking dish. Cook, uncovered, with the microwave on HIGH for 10 minutes. Combine the orange juice and browning sauce in a cup. Brush the duck with this orange mixture. Return to the microwave and continue cooking on HIGH for 10 minutes. Brush the duck with the orange mixture and continue cooking on HIGH for 10 minutes. Turn the duck, breast side up, and remove the foil from the wings and legs; then brush with the remaining orange mixture or pan drippings. Return to the microwave and continue cooking on MEDIUM for 15 minutes or until the drumstick feels soft; while cooking, brush the duck occasionally with the pan drippings. Remove from the oven; then cover with aluminum foil or allow to rest for 15 minutes in a warm oven before serving.

Yield: 20 servings
Exchange, 1 serving: 2¼ high-fat meat, 1 fruit
Calories, 1 serving: 394
Carbohydrates, 1 serving: 16

Duck with Sauerkraut

5 lb.	duck	2½ kg
	salt and pepper	
2 qts.	sauerkraut	2 L
3 T.	granulated sugar replacement	45 mL

Wash the duck and trim the fat; discard the giblets. Salt and pepper both the outside and cavity of the duck. Cover the ends of the wings and legs with aluminum foil. Tie the wings and legs to the body with cotton thread. Prick the skin several places with a sharp fork. Place the duck, breast side down, on a roasting rack in a baking dish. Cook, uncovered, with the microwave on HIGH for 30 minutes, rotating the dish a quarter turn every 10 minutes. Turn the duck, breast side up, and remove the foil from the wings and legs. Cover with the sauerkraut and sprinkle with the sugar replacement. Cover with wax paper. Return to the microwave and continue on MEDIUM for 15 minutes or until the drumstick feels soft. Remove from the oven; then remove the wax paper and cover with aluminum foil. Allow to rest for 15 minutes before serving.

Yield: 20 servings
Exchange, 1 serving: 2¼ high-fat meat, ½ vegetable
Calories, 1 serving: 342
Carbohydrates, 1 serving: 3

Chestnut Duck

3 lb.	duck, cut up	1½ kg
2 c.	boiling water	500 mL
6 c.	chestnuts	1500 mL
2 c.	sliced mushrooms	500 mL
¼ c.	soy sauce	60 mL
	pepper	

Wash the duck and cut it into smaller serving-size pieces. Place the duck in a 3 qt. (3 L) microwave casserole or baking dish. Cover with the 2 c. (500 mL) boiling water. Then cover with a lid or plastic wrap. With the microwave on HIGH, cook for 25 minutes. Meanwhile, drop the chestnuts into cold water in a 3 qt. (3 L) microwave dish or saucepan. Discard any chestnuts that float. With the microwave on HIGH, cook for 10 minutes—or bring the water to boiling in a saucepan on top of the stove, reduce the heat, and simmer for 5 minutes. Drain the water and then peel the chestnuts. Now, remove the duck from the microwave and drain off any fat and liquid. Add the cooked chestnuts, mushrooms, soy sauce, and pepper to the duck. Cover and return to the microwave. Cook on MEDIUM for 20 minutes.

Yield: 10 servings
Exchange, 1 serving: 2½ high-fat meat, ½ vegetable
Calories, 1 serving: 408
Carbohydrates, 1 serving: 3

Roast Goose

8 lb.	goose	4 kg
2 qts.	dry bread crumbs	2 L
2	onions, chopped	2
2 t.	sage	20 mL
2 t.	salt	10 mL
¼. t.	pepper	1 mL
	water	

Wash and remove any fat from the goose. Salt the inside of the body and neck cavities. Combine the remaining ingredients, using just enough water to lightly moisten the bread cubes. Place this stuffing into the goose cavities. Secure with toothpicks. Secure the wings and legs with toothpicks or plastic poultry pins. Place the goose, breast side down, on a microwave roasting rack in a baking dish. With the microwave on HIGH, cook for 20 minutes; then reduce the heat and rotate the dish one-half turn. Continue cooking with the microwave on MEDIUM for 15 minutes. Turn the goose over, breast side up, and continue cooking on MEDIUM for 45 minutes or until the drumstick is soft. Cover with aluminum foil or place in a warm oven to rest for 10 minutes.

Yield: 20 servings
Exchange, 1 serving: 2⅔ high-fat meat, ½ bread
Calories, 1 serving: 431
Carbohydrates, 1 serving: 7

Roast Turkey

12 lb.	whole young turkey	6 kg
	salt and pepper	
	stuffing, if desired	
3 T.	browning and seasoning sauce	45 mL
1 T.	Worcestershire sauce	15 mL
1 T.	water	15 mL
1 T.	reduced-calorie margarine, melted	15 mL

Thaw a frozen turkey completely. Wash the outside of the turkey and inside both cavities. Discard the giblets, unless you will be using them in stuffing. Sprinkle the cavities with salt and pepper. Stuff the cavities, if desired. Secure the cavities, wings, and legs with toothpicks or tie with cotton string. Cover the ends of the wing tips and legs with aluminum foil. Place the turkey, breast side down, on a microwave roasting rack in a 4 qt. (4 L) baking dish. Combine the browning sauce, Worcestershire sauce, water, and margarine in a small bowl. Brush the bottom of the turkey with this browning mixture. With the microwave on HIGH, cook, uncovered, for 30 minutes; rotate the dish a quarter turn every 5 to 7 minutes, and check the turkey and brush it with the browning mixture occasionally. If any areas on the turkey appear to be cooking too rapidly, cover them with paper towels. Return the turkey to the microwave and continue cooking on MEDIUM for 30 minutes. Remove any paper towels and turn the turkey over, breast side up. Brush with the browning mixture, and rotate the dish to coat the turkey completely with the mixture. With the microwave on MEDIUM, cook for 30 more minutes or until the thigh feels soft. Allow to rest for 15 minutes covered with aluminum foil or in a warm oven.

Yield: 30 servings
Exchange, (without stuffing) 1 serving: 3 lean meat
Calories, (without stuffing) 1 serving: 192
Carbohydrates, (without stuffing) 1 serving: negligible

Turkey Drumsticks

2 lb.	turkey drumsticks	1 kg
½ c.	water	125 mL
1	bay leaf	1
½ t.	thyme	2 mL
½ t.	sage	2 mL
	salt and pepper	

Wash the drumsticks thoroughly. Place the drumsticks with their thick end towards the outside of a 2 qt. (2 L) microwave baking dish. Add the remaining ingredients. Cover with plastic wrap. With the microwave on HIGH, cook for 10 minutes. Rotate the dish a quarter turn and continue cooking on MEDIUM for 15 minutes. Turn the drumsticks over, baste with the dish drippings, and add extra water if needed. Re-cover and return to the microwave. Cook on MEDIUM for 20 minutes or until the meat is fork-tender.

Yield: 10 servings
Exchange, 1 serving: 2 lean meat
Calories, 1 serving: 115
Carbohydrates, 1 serving: negligible

Fish

Swordfish Royal

¼ c.	water	60 mL
1 t.	browning and seasoning sauce	5 mL
½ lb.	swordfish steak	250 g
1 T.	grated carrot	15 mL
1 T.	finely diced onion	15 mL
1 T.	finely chopped parsley	15 mL
1 T.	very thinly sliced celery	15 mL

Combine the water and browning sauce in an 8 in. (20 cm) pie plate. Place the swordfish steak in the plate; then turn over once to coat both sides. Cover tightly with plastic wrap. With the microwave on MEDIUM, cook for 2 minutes. Turn the steak over. Cook on MEDIUM for 2 more minutes. Place the vegetables around the side of the pie plate. Cover and cook on MEDIUM for 2 additional minutes.

Yield: 2 servings
Exchange, 1 serving: 2 medium-fat meat
Calories, 1 serving: 135
Carbohydrates, 1 serving: negligible

Salmon Superb

1 T.	reduced-calorie margarine	15 mL
½ t.	lemon juice	2 mL
1 T.	chopped chives	15 mL
½ t.	basil	2 mL
½ lb.	salmon steak	250 g

Melt the margarine in an 8 in. (20 cm) pie plate. Stir in the lemon juice, chives, and basil. Place the salmon steak in a pie plate and turn over once to coat both sides with the mixture. Cover with plastic wrap. With the microwave on MEDIUM, cook for 2 minutes. Turn the plate one-half rotation. Cook on MEDIUM for 2 more minutes. Turn the plate one-quarter rotation, and cook 2 minutes longer.

Yield: 2 servings
Exchange, 1 serving: 3 medium-fat meat
Calories, 1 serving: 236
Carbohydrates, 1 serving: negligible

Fillets of Sole with Vegetables

2 T.	reduced-calorie margarine	30 mL
1 qt.	thinly sliced potatoes	1 L
2 c.	minced onion	500 mL
¼ t.	white pepper	2 mL
⅓ c.	minced parsley	90 mL
2 lbs. (8 fillets)	sole fillets	1 kg (8 fillets)
1 c.	plain yogurt	250 mL
1 large	egg	1 large
¼ c.	shredded sharp Cheddar cheese	60 mL

Melt the margarine in a 13 × 9 in. (33 × 23 cm) baking dish. Add the potatoes and onions; then sprinkle with white pepper. Cover with plastic wrap. With the microwave on HIGH, cook for 2 minutes. Stir in ¼ c. (60 mL) of the parsley. Remove half of the vegetables and set them aside. Rinse the fillets in salted water, and pat them dry with paper towels. Arrange the fish on top of the vegetables in the baking dish. Combine the yogurt and egg in a bowl, and thoroughly blend. Pour half of this mixture over the fish. Top with the vegetables that were set aside. Add the cheese to the remaining yogurt mixture and pour over the top. Sprinkle with the remaining parsley. Cover with plastic wrap. With the microwave on MEDIUM, cook for 5 to 6 minutes, turning the dish one-half rotation every 2 minutes or until the fish is tender.

Yield: 8 servings
Exchange, 1 serving: 1½ medium-fat meat, ¾ bread
Calories, 1 serving: 167
Carbohydrates, 1 serving: 11

Orange Roughy with Mushroom-Cheese Sauce

½ lb. (2 fillets)	orange roughy fillets	250 g (2 fillets)
½ c.	sliced mushrooms	125 mL
10 oz. can	cream of mushroom soup	285 g can
3 T.	Cheddar cheese soup	45 mL
	water	
Optional:		
1T.	chopped chives	15 mL
1T.	chopped pimiento or red pepper	15 mL

Clean the fillets and cut them in half. Place the fillets in a single layer in a shallow microwave baking dish with the thick edge of the fillet to the outside. Top with the sliced mushrooms. Cover with wax paper. With the microwave on HIGH, cook for 2 minutes. Drain off any excess liquid. Combine the soups with just enough water to make a sauce with a thick pouring consistency. Pour over the fillets. Cook, uncovered, in the microwave for 3 to 4 minutes or until the fillets flake easily with a fork. If desired, garnish with chives and pimiento just before serving.

Yield: 4 servings
Exchange, 1 serving: 1 medium-fat meat, ½ bread
Calories, 1 serving: 114
Carbohydrates, 1 serving: 8

Halibut Steaks with Broccoli-Fennel Sauce

½ c.	dry white wine	125 mL
½ c.	water	125 mL
½ c.	finely chopped onion	125 mL
¼ c.	finely grated carrot	60 mL
1 T.	parsley flakes	15 mL
1 t.	Worcestershire sauce	5 mL
¼ t.	salt	1 mL
dash	black pepper	dash
1½ lb. (4 steaks)	halibut steaks	750 g (4 steaks)
10 oz. pkg.	frozen broccoli, thawed	265 g pkg.
½ t.	fennel seed, crushed	2 mL
½ c.	reduced-calorie mayonnaise	125 mL
1 T.	Dijon mustard	15 mL

Combine the wine, water, onion, carrot, parsley, Worcestershire sauce, salt, and pepper in a shallow microwave dish. With the microwave on

HIGH, cook for 3 to 4 minutes or until boiling. Lay the halibut steaks in a single layer on the bottom of the dish. Cover with wax paper. With the microwave on MEDIUM, cook for 3 to 4 minutes or until the fish flakes easily with a fork. Remove the bones and skin from the steaks. Keep warm in the liquid. Meanwhile, combine the broccoli and fennel in a food processor; then process with a steel blade until the broccoli is completely chopped. Turn into a microwave dish. Add the remaining ingredients, stirring to blend. Cover with wax paper, and cook with the microwave on HIGH for 1½ minutes. Stir and continue cooking on HIGH for 30 seconds. Place the halibut steaks on a serving platter or on individual plates, and top with the broccoli-fennel sauce.

Yield: 6 servings
Exchange, 1 serving: 1½ medium-fat meat, ½ vegetable
Calories, 1 serving: 131
Carbohydrates, 1 serving: 3

Rainbow Trout

or other trout about 8 oz. (240 g)

8 oz.	whole trout	240 g
2 T.	reduced-calorie margarine, melted	30 mL
1 T.	lemon juice	15 mL
	salt, pepper, and paprika	

Clean and wash the trout thoroughly, leaving the head and tail in place. Cover the head and tail with aluminum foil. Place the trout on a shallow microwave baking dish. Combine the margarine, lemon juice, salt, pepper, and paprika in a small bowl. Lightly brush the outside skin of the trout. Cover with plastic wrap. With the microwave on HIGH, cook for 2 minutes. Carefully remove the plastic wrap; then turn the fish over and brush with the margarine mixture. Cover lightly with wax paper. With the microwave on HIGH, cook for 3 minutes. Allow the trout to rest for 4 to 5 minutes before serving. (Allow 2 to 3 extra minutes for each additional trout cooked at the same time. The trout should flake easily with a fork.)

Yield: 1 serving
Exchange: 2 lean meat, 2 fat
Calories: 201
Carbohydrates: negligible

Fillet of Sole Amandine

2 lbs. (8 fillets)	sole fillets	1 kg (8 fillets)
3 T.	water	45 mL
2 T.	reduced-calorie margarine	30 mL
⅓ c.	slivered almonds	90 mL
1 T.	dry white wine	15 mL
2 t.	lemon juice	10 mL
½ t.	salt	2 mL
¼ t.	minced garlic	1 mL
	white pepper	

Rinse the fish in salted water. Pour the 3 T. (45 mL) water into a 13 × 9 in. (33 × 23 cm) baking dish. Arrange the fish fillets on the bottom of the dish, and cover with plastic wrap. With the microwave on MEDIUM, cook for 3 minutes, turning the dish one-half rotation after 1½ minutes. Drain the fish thoroughly of any excess liquid and set aside. Place the margarine in a microwave dish. Melt in the microwave on MEDIUM or MEDIUM HIGH. Add the almonds, wine, lemon juice, salt, and garlic. With the microwave on MEDIUM, cook for 1½ minutes. Pour over the fish fillets, cover with plastic wrap, and cook on MEDIUM in the microwave for 2 minutes. Sprinkle with white pepper and parsley.

Yield: 8 servings
Exchange, 1 serving: 1½ medium-fat meat
Calories, 1 serving: 113
Carbohydrates, 1 serving: negligible

Stuffed Whitefish

1 lb.	dressed whole whitefish	500 g
2 T.	reduced-calorie margarine	30 mL
½ t.	salt	2 mL
3 T.	minced onion	45 mL
2 T.	water	30 mL
1½ c.	seasoned bread cubes	375 mL
	paprika	

Wash the fish and pat it dry with paper towels. Melt the margarine in a medium-sized microwave bowl. Brush the inside of the fish cavity with 2 t. of the melted margarine; then salt the cavity. Combine the remaining melted margarine, onions, and water. Cook in the microwave, uncovered, on HIGH for 1 minute. Thoroughly stir in the seasoned bread cubes. Fill the cavity of the fish with the stuffing. Lace the cavity closed, using wooden toothpicks and string. Sprinkle the fish with paprika. Place the fish on a microwave platter, and cover with plastic wrap. With the microwave on MEDIUM, cook for 10 to 12 minutes. Turn the fish over after 5 minutes, and sprinkle the outside of the fish with paprika. Continue cooking on MEDIUM for 5 to 7 minutes or until the fish flakes easily with a fork.

Yield: 4 servings
Exchange, 1 serving: 1½ medium-fat meat, 1 bread
Calories, 1 serving: 203
Carbohydrates, 1 serving: 14

Poached Sole

1 lb.	sole fillets	500 g
½ c.	white wine	125 mL
½ c.	water	125 mL
3 small	sprigs of parsley	3 small
1	carrot, sliced	1
1 stalk	celery, sliced	1
1	onion, sliced	1
1	bay leaf	1
½ t.	ground thyme	2 mL

Wash the sole fillets in salted water, and pat them dry with paper towels. Combine the remaining ingredients in a 3 qt. (3 L) casserole or baking dish with a cover. Cook this mixture in the covered dish on HIGH in the microwave for 7 minutes or until boiling. Allow the mixture to set for 5 minutes so that the flavors can combine. This mixture may be used for other recipes. If the liquid has reduced, add equal amounts of wine and water to it. Then lay the sole fillets in the mixture. Cover and cook in the microwave on MEDIUM for 5 minutes or until the fillets flake easily with a fork. Carefully lift the fillets out of the dish with two spatulas. Lay the fillets on a serving dish and pat them dry with paper towels. If desired, sprinkle with paprika and trim with lemon slices.

Yield: 4 servings
Exchange, 1 serving: 1⅓ lean meat
Calories, 1 serving: 73
Carbohydrates, 1 serving: 1

Simplified Seafood

½ c.	white wine	125 mL
½ c.	water	125 mL
3 small	sprigs of parsley	3 small
1	carrot, sliced	1
1 stalk	celery, sliced	1
1	onion, sliced	1
1	bay leaf	1
½ t.	ground thyme	2 mL
6 large	uncooked shrimp, peeled	6 large
12	fresh mussels	12
6 (3 oz. each)	sole fillets	6 (90 g each)
2 T.	reduced-calorie margarine	30 mL
¼ lb.	fresh mushrooms, sliced	125 g
3 T.	chopped green onions	45 mL
	parsley sprigs	

Combine the wine, water, parsley, carrot, celery, onion, bay leaf, and ground thyme in a 3 qt. (3 L) casserole or baking dish with a cover. With the microwave on HIGH, cook this liquid mixture, covered, for 7 minutes or until boiling. Allow the mixture to set for 5 minutes to allow the flavors to combine; then remove the parsley sprigs. (This mixture may be used for other recipes. If the mixture has reduced, add equal amounts of wine and water to it.) Add the shrimp and cook, covered, on HIGH in the microwave for 2 minutes or until the shrimp are pink. Remove the shrimp and add the mussels. Cook, covered, with the microwave on MEDIUM for 2 minutes or until the shells are open. Remove the mussels. Wash the sole fillets in salted water and lay them in the liquid. Cover and cook with the microwave on MEDIUM for 3 minutes or until the fillets flake easily with a fork. Carefully lift the fillets out of the dish with two spatulas. Keep the shrimp, mussels, and fillets warm in a heated oven. Melt the margarine in a medium-sized microwave bowl. Add the mushrooms and green onions. With the microwave on HIGH, cook for 3 minutes. Place a shrimp, two mussels, and a sole fillet on six serving plates; decorate with parsley.

Yield: 6 servings
Exchange, 1 serving: 2 lean meat
Calories, 1 serving: 118
Carbohydrates, 1 serving: negligible

Salmon Parmigiana

1 lb. can	salmon	458 g can
¼ c.	ketchup	60 mL
2 t.	mustard	10 mL
2 t.	Worcestershire sauce	10 mL
1 slice	white bread	1 slice

Pour the liquid from the salmon into a medium-size bowl. Place the salmon on a plate and carefully remove the bones and skin, if desired. Add the ketchup, mustard, and Worcestershire sauce to the salmon liquid. Cut or break the bread into small pieces; then add to the liquid. Stir to blend. Carefully fold the salmon into the liquid; try not to mash the salmon. Pile it into four seafood shells or the middle of small plates. Cover with plastic wrap. With the microwave on MEDIUM HIGH, cook for 4 minutes. Carefully remove the plastic wrap, and serve.

Yield: 4 servings
Exchange, 1 serving: 2 medium-fat meat
Calories, 1 serving: 164
Carbohydrates, 1 serving: 4

Breaded Ocean Perch Fillets

1 lb. pkg.	frozen perch fillets, thawed	500 g pkg
2 oz. pkg	seasoned coating mix for fish	60 g pkg

Clean the perch fillets thoroughly; then wash and pat dry. Cover with the seasoned coating mix. Shake off any excess. Place the fillets in a single layer on a shallow microwave baking dish, with the thickest part of the fish towards the outside. Cover with wax paper. With the microwave on HIGH, cook for 6 to 7 minutes or until the fish flakes easily with a fork; rotate the dish a quarter turn after 2 minutes, then every 2 minutes.

Yield: 4 servings
Exchange, 1 serving: 1 medium-fat meat, 1 bread
Calories, 1 serving: 155
Carbohydrates, 1 serving: 16

Flounder in Tomato Sauce

2 lbs.	flounder fillets	1 kg
6 oz. can	tomato paste	180 g can
¾ c.	water	190 mL
½ c.	chopped onions	125 mL
2 cloves	garlic, sliced	2 cloves
1½ T.	lime juice	21 mL
1	bay leaf, crushed	1
½ t.	oregano	2 mL
¼ t.	thyme	1 mL
¼ t.	salt	1 mL
⅛ t.	black pepper	½ mL

Clean and wash the flounder fillets, and pat them dry. Place the fillets in a lightly greased 9 × 13 in. (23 × 33 cm) microwave baking dish. Combine the remaining ingredients in a bowl, stirring to mix. Allow this tomato mixture to rest for 5 minutes. Then pour the tomato mixture over the fish. Cover with plastic wrap. With the microwave on HIGH, cook for 3 minutes. Carefully remove the plastic wrap. Continue cooking on HIGH for 5 to 6 minutes, rotating the dish one-half turn after 5½ minutes. Remove from the microwave, and cover with aluminum foil or keep warm in a heated oven for 5 minutes before serving.

Yield: 8 servings
Exchange, 1 serving: 1½ lean meat, 1 vegetable
Calories, 1 serving: 115
Carbohydrates, 1 serving: 3

South Seas Sole

1½ lbs.	sole fillets	750 g
6 oz. can	tomato paste	180 g can
½ c.	water	125 mL
1½ t.	lime juice	7 mL
1 t.	coconut flavoring	5 mL
½ t.	nutmeg	2 mL
½ t.	onion flakes	2 mL

Wash and clean the sole fillets. Lightly oil a shallow microwave baking dish with nonstick cooking spray. Place the fish fillets on the bottom of the baking dish. Combine the remaining ingredients in a bowl, stirring to completely blend. Pour over the sole. Place two layers of paper towels on top of the dish. With the microwave on MEDIUM, cook for 10 to 15 minutes or until the fish flakes easily with a fork. Turn the dish twice during cooking.

Yield: 4 servings
Exchange, 1 serving: 2 lean meat, 2 vegetable
Calories, 1 serving: 175
Carbohydrates, 1 serving: 9

Cold Whitefish

3 lb.	whole whitefish	1½ kg
1 T.	lemon juice	15 mL
2 c.	water	500 mL
½ c.	white wine	125 mL
5	green onions, finely chopped	5
1 clove	garlic, minced	1 clove
1 small	leek, finely chopped	1 small
2	carrots, finely chopped	2
2 sprigs	parsley, finely chopped	2 sprigs
1	bay leaf, crushed	1
½ t.	salt	2 mL
½ t.	white pepper	2 mL

Clean the whitefish, leaving the head and tail intact. Sprinkle the cavity and outside with the lemon juice; then wrap the fish in plastic wrap and place it in a shallow microwave dish. Refrigerate at least 1 hour. Combine the remaining ingredients in a 2 qt. (2 L) microwave bowl or measuring cup. With the microwave on HIGH, cook for 5 to 7 minutes or until boiling. Allow the mixture to rest until cool. Remove the plastic wrap from the whitefish. Pour this cool mixture over the fish. Cover with wax paper. With the microwave on HIGH, cook for 3 minutes. Turn the fish over, re-cover, and continue cooking in the microwave on MEDIUM for 7 to 10 minutes. Allow the fish to rest in the liquid mixture for 3 to 4 minutes or until the fish flakes easily with a fork. Remove the fish from the liquid, allow to cool, and then refrigerate until cold. To serve: Remove the skin but leave the head and tail intact.

Yield: 6 servings
Exchange, 1 serving: 1 lean meat
Calories, 1 serving: 61
Carbohydrates, 1 serving: negligible

Seafood

Garlic Shrimp

2 lbs.	large unshelled raw shrimp, deveined	1 kg
½ c.	reduced-calorie dressing	125 mL
¼ c.	finely chopped parsley	60 mL
3 cloves	garlic, sliced	3 cloves
1½ T.	lemon juice	21 mL
1 T.	minced green onion	15 mL
1 t.	salt	5 mL

Wash the shrimp in cold water and pat dry. Combine the remaining ingredients in a 3 qt. (3 L) microwave casserole or baking dish. Stir to mix completely. Add the shrimp and fold in to completely coat. Cover with a lid or plastic wrap. Marinate at room temperature 30 minutes before cooking. Then remove the lid or plastic wrap, and cover with paper towels. With the microwave on HIGH, cook for 5 to 7 minutes or until the meat of the shrimp turns white and opaque; rearrange the shrimp every 2 minutes while cooking. Allow to rest 4 minutes before serving. To serve, remove the shrimp with a slotted spoon.

Yield: 10 servings
Exchange, 1 serving: 1 lean meat, ¼ fat
Calories, 1 serving: 65
Carbohydrates, 1 serving: negligible

Shrimp and Crab with Madeira

1 T.	reduced-calorie margarine	15 mL
3 T.	chopped green onions	45 mL
½ c.	sliced mushrooms	125 mL

½ lb.	shrimp, uncooked	250 g
½ lb.	crabmeat	250 g
½ c.	Madeira	125 mL
1 T.	lemon juice	15 mL
1 T.	tomato paste	15 mL
	salt and pepper to taste	

Melt the margarine in a 1 c. (250 mL) measuring cup. Add the green onions and mushrooms. Cover with plastic wrap. With the microwave on HIGH, cook for 2 minutes. Combine the shrimp and crab in a 2 qt. (2 L) microwave casserole or baking dish. Stir in the vegetables. Cover with a lid or plastic wrap. With the microwave on HIGH, cook for 3 minutes. Combine the Madeira, lemon juice, and tomato paste; stir then to blend. Stir this Madeira mixture into a shrimp-crab mixture. Return to the microwave, uncovered, and cook on MEDIUM for 5 to 6 minutes, stirring every 2 minutes. Add salt and pepper to taste.

Yield: 4 servings
Exchange, 1 serving: 2 lean meat, ¼ bread
Calories, 1 serving: 130
Carbohydrates, 1 serving: 4

Lobster Tails

8 oz.	lobster tail	238 g
1 T.	reduced-calorie margarine, melted	15 mL
	paprika	

The lobster tail should be fresh or unfrozen. Place the lobster, with the flesh side up and the thick end to the outside, in a microwave plate or platter. Brush with melted margarine, and sprinkle with paprika. Cover with plastic wrap. With the microwave on HIGH, cook for 3 to 4 minutes. Allow the lobster to rest 3 minutes before serving. The lobster should have a red shell and its flesh should be white and opaque. Allow 2 extra minutes of cooking and resting time for each additional lobster tail.

Yield: 1 serving
Exchange, 1 serving: 1 lean meat, 1 fat
Calories, 1 serving: 99
Carbohydrates, 1 serving: negligible

Crab Patties

½ lb.	crabmeat	250 g
¼ c.	minced parsley	60 mL
1 t.	dill seed, crushed	5 mL
1 t.	cumin	5 mL
1 t.	ginger	5 mL
1 t.	salt	5 mL
½ t.	nutmeg	2 mL
1 c.	soft bread crumbs	250 mL
2 oz	seasoned coating mix for fish	68 g

Combine the crabmeat, parsley, dill seed, cumin, ginger, salt, and nutmeg in a mixing bowl. Blend completely. Add the bread crumbs, and mix thoroughly. Form into 12 patties. Chill the patties at least 2 hours. Lay the patties on a piece of wax paper. Sprinkle both sides with the coating mix. Place the patties on a microwave platter. Cover with wax paper. With the microwave on HIGH, cook for 4 to 5 minutes; while cooking, rotate the dish a quarter turn after 1 minute, then every 30 seconds.

Yield: 4 servings
Exchange, 1 serving: 1 lean meat, ¼ bread
Calories, 1 serving: 73
Carbohydrates, 1 serving: 4

Scallop Kabob

1	green pepper	1
24 (about 2 lbs.)	large sea scallops	24 (about 1 kg)
1 T.	Worcestershire sauce	15 mL
1 T.	water	15 mL

Cut the green pepper into 24 squares or pieces. Place the green pepper squares in a shallow microwave dish. With the microwave on HIGH, cook for 1 minute or until crisp-tender. Wash the scallops and pat them dry. Place a pepper square on a skewer, follow with a scallop; alternate this way until each skewer has four of each. Six skewers are used. Combine the Worcestershire sauce and water in a cup. Brush the kabobs lightly with the Worcestershire mixture. Lay the skewers across an 8 in. (20 cm)-square baking dish. Cover lightly with wax paper. With the microwave on HIGH, cook for 8 to 10 minutes or until the scallops are done.

Yield: 6 servings
Exchange, 1 serving: 2 lean meat
Calories, 1 serving: 112
Carbohydrates, 1 serving: negligible

Scallops Cilantro

1 T.	olive oil	15 mL
½ c.	chopped onion	125 mL
¼ c.	chopped green pepper	60 mL
1 clove	garlic, minced	1 clove
1 small	bay leaf	1 small
½ t.	oregano	1 mL
⅛ t.	thyme	½ mL
⅛ t.	hot red pepper	½ mL
4	tomatoes, finely chopped	4
6 oz. can	tomato sauce	240 g can
1 lb	bay scallops	500 g
2 T.	chopped fresh cilantro	30 mL
	salt	

With the microwave on HIGH, heat the oil in a 2 qt. (2 L) microwave casserole or baking dish for 1 minute. Stir in the onion, green pepper, and garlic. With the microwave on MEDIUM, cook for 2 to 3 minutes. Stir in the bay leaf, oregano, thyme, and hot red pepper. Continue cooking on MEDIUM for 2 minutes. Stir in the tomatoes and tomato sauce. Cover with a lid or plastic wrap. With the microwave on HIGH, cook for 2 minutes or until the sauce is boiling; then stir, reduce the heat to LOW, and continue cooking for 5 to 6 minutes. Add the scallops and cook them for 1 minute. Stir in the cilantro; then add salt to taste. Cover and allow to rest for 5 minutes. Check the mixture for temperature and the scallops for doneness; if needed, return to the microwave and cook on MEDIUM for 1 minute.

Yield: 6 servings
Exchange, 1 serving: 1 medium-fat meat, 1 vegetable
Calories, 1 serving: 101
Carbohydrates, 1 serving: 6

Shrimp Curry

10 oz. can	cream of shrimp soup	285 g can
¼ c.	cream of mushroom soup	60 mL
¼ c.	water	60 mL
2 T.	chopped green onion	30 mL
1 T.	lemon juice	15 mL
1 t.	curry powder	5 mL
8 oz.	frozen cooked shrimp, thawed	240 mL

Combine the soups, water, green onion, lemon juice, and curry powder in a 2 qt. (2 L) microwave casserole or baking dish. Stir to mix. With the microwave on HIGH, cook, uncovered, for 5 minutes, stirring after 2 minutes. Stir in the shrimp and continue cooking with the microwave on MEDIUM for 2 to 3 minutes.

Yield: 4 servings
Exchange, 1 serving: 1 lean meat, 1 bread, ¼ fat
Calories, 1 serving: 143
Carbohydrates, 1 serving: 16

Sweet and Sour Shrimp

1 c.	crushed pineapple, in its own juice	250 mL
2 T.	finely chopped onion	30 mL
3 T.	vinegar	45 mL
1 T.	cornstarch	15 mL
dash	salt	dash
12 oz.	frozen cooked shrimp, thawed	360 g

Combine the pineapple (with its juice), onion, vinegar, cornstarch, and salt in a 1½ qt. (1½ L) microwave casserole or baking dish. With the microwave on HIGH, cook for 4 to 5 minutes or until thickened; stir after 2 minutes, then every 30 seconds. Stir in the drained shrimp. With the microwave on HIGH, cook for 2 minutes or until the shrimp flesh is white; stir about 1 minute. Allow the mixture to rest for 4 minutes before serving.

Yield: 4 servings
Exchange, 1 serving: 1 lean meat, 1 fruit
Calories, 1 serving: 117
Carbohydrates, 1 serving: 13

Mexican Lobster

2 T.	reduced-calorie margarine	30 mL
1 qt.	tomatoes, finely chopped	1 L
1 c.	sliced mushrooms	250 mL
1	onion, finely chopped	1
1	green pepper, finely chopped	1
½ t.	salt	2 mL
¼ t.	ground cloves	1 mL
1	bay leaf	1
2 c.	diced cooked lobster	500 mL
dash	hot pepper sauce	dash

Melt the margarine in a 2 qt. (2 L) microwave casserole or baking dish. Add the tomatoes, mushrooms, onion, green pepper, salt, ground cloves, and bay leaf. Cover with a lid or plastic wrap. With the microwave on HIGH, cook for 5 to 6 minutes or until the mixture becomes a sauce; stir occasionally. Allow to rest 5 minutes before proceeding. Remove the bay leaf. Stir in the lobster and hot pepper sauce. Return to the microwave, uncovered, and cook on HIGH for 2 to 3 minutes or until the lobster is hot.

Yield: 8 servings
Exchange, 1 serving: 1 lean meat, 1 vegetable, ½ fat
Calories, 1 serving: 103
Carbohydrates, 1 serving: 6

Seasoned Bay Scallops

| 1 lb. | bay scallops | 500 g |
| ¼ c. | reduced-calorie French dressing | 60 mL |

Marinate the scallops in the French dressing for 2 to 3 hours. Arrange in a single layer in the bottom of a shallow microwave dish or pie pan. Cover with damp paper towels. With the microwave on HIGH, cook for 1 minute. Then rearrange the scallops and continue cooking for 1 or 2 minute(s) or until the scallops are done.

Yield: 4 servings
Exchange, 1 serving: 1½ medium-fat meat
Calories, 1 serving: 97
Carbohydrates, 1 serving: negligible

Eggs & Cheese

Soft- or Hard-Cooked Eggs

Break the egg into a microwave or glass custard cup. Prick the yolk and cover with plastic wrap. For one or two egg(s), place the cup(s) off-center in the microwave oven; for three or more eggs, place the cups in a circle on a flat plate in the microwave oven. (A food rotator is recommended for soft- and hard-cooked eggs.) With the microwave on ME-DIUM, cook for the amount of time given below (these times are approximate). Allow the eggs to rest for 3 minutes before serving.

Soft:

# of eggs	Time
1	40 to 45 seconds
2	45 to 50 seconds
3	1½ minutes to 2 minutes
4	2½ minutes to 3 minutes

Hard:

1	1 minute
2	1 minute 15 seconds
3	2 to 2½ minutes
4	3 to 3½ minutes

Exchange, 1 egg: 1 medium-fat meat
Calories, 1 egg: 80
Carbohydrates, 1 egg: negligible

Poached Eggs

For one or two eggs:
Use individual microwave or glass custard cups. Combine ¼ c. (60 mL) of hot tap water and ¼ t. (1 mL) of vinegar in each cup. With the microwave on HIGH, cook for 2 minutes or until the water is rapidly boiling. Break one egg at a time onto a small saucer, and carefully slip it into the boiling water. Cover with plastic wrap. Return to the microwave and continue cooking on MEDIUM for 30 to 45 seconds per egg.

For three or four eggs:

1c.	hot tap water	250 mL.
½ t.	vinegar	2 mL.
	eggs	

Combine the water and vinegar in a 1 qt. (1 L) microwave casserole or baking dish. With the microwave on HIGH, cook for 2 to 3 minutes or until the water is rapidly boiling. Carefully break the eggs into the boiling water or use the method above. Cover with a lid or plastic wrap. Return to the microwave and continue cooking on MEDIUM for 2½ to 3 minutes or until the whites are almost set. Allow the eggs to rest a few minutes before serving.

Exchange, 1 egg: 1 medium-fat meat
Calories, 1 egg: 80
Carbohydrates 1 egg: negligible

Scrambled Eggs

Combine the eggs and 1 T. (15 mL) of skim milk for each egg used (four eggs is the maximum number recommended in the microwave) in a microwave casserole or baking dish that has been sprayed with vegetable oil. Beat well with fork or whisk. Season with salt and pepper. Cover with a lid or plastic wrap. With the microwave on MEDIUM, cook for 1 minute for each egg being prepared—such as, one egg for 1 minute, two eggs for 2 minutes, etc.

Exchange, 1 egg: 1 medium-fat meat
Calories, 1 egg: 80
Carbohydrates, 1 egg: negligible

Breakfast Bake

12 oz.	frozen hash browns	343 g
⅓ c.	skim milk	90 mL
2 t.	cornstarch	10 mL
½	salt	2 mL
	black pepper to taste	
2 T.	imitation bacon bits	30 mL
1 T.	chopped onion	15 mL
4	eggs	4

Grease the bottom and sides of a 2 qt. (2 L) microwave casserole or baking dish with vegetable oil spray. Add the hash browns; then cover with a lid or plastic wrap. With the microwave on HIGH, cook 6 to 7 minutes or until the hash browns are partially soft. Dissolve the cornstarch in the milk. Stir into the hash browns. Add the salt, pepper, bacon bits, and onion. Stir to completely mix. Make four indentations in the hash browns. Break one egg into each indentation. Re-cover and return to the microwave. Continue cooking on MEDIUM for 6 to 8 minutes or until the eggs are almost cooked to desired doneness. Allow the mixture to rest 2 minutes before serving.

Yield: 4 servings
Exchange, 1 serving: 1 bread, 1 medium-fat meat
Calories, 1 serving: 143
Carbohydrates, 1 serving: 18

Spanish Eggs

4	eggs	4
⅓ c.	chopped tomatoes	90 mL
¼ c.	shredded Cheddar cheese	60 mL
2 T.	finely chopped green pepper	30 mL
1 T.	finely chopped onion	15 mL
¼ t.	Worcestershire sauce	1 mL
⅛ t.	Tabasco sauce	1 mL
	salt and pepper to taste	

Beat the eggs until completely mixed. Combine the eggs and other ingredients in a greased 1½ qt. (1½ L) microwave casserole or baking dish. Stir to mix. Cook, uncovered, with the microwave on HIGH for 3 to 4 minutes or until the mixture is almost set; rotate the dish one-half turn and stir after 2 minutes, then every 60 seconds. Remove from the oven, cover, and allow the mixture to rest for 3 to 4 minutes before serving.

Yield: 4 servings
Exchange, 1 serving: 1⅓ medium-fat meat
Calories, 1 serving: 109
Carbohydrates, 1 serving: 2

Quiche Lorraine

10 slices	bacon	10 slices
1 c.	shredded Cheddar cheese	250 mL
⅓ c.	finely chopped onion	90 mL
1 c.	skim milk	250 mL
3	eggs	3
½ t.	salt	2 mL
⅛ t.	black pepper	½ mL
Optional:		
9 in.	baked pastry shell in pie dish	23 cm

Place the bacon slices on a roast rack in a 13 × 9 in. (33 × 23 cm) microwave baking dish. Cover with two layers of paper towels. With the microwave on HIGH, cook for 6 to 8 minutes or until the bacon is crisp. Cool completely. Crumble the bacon on the bottom of 9 in. (23 cm) pie pan or prepared pastry shell. Sprinkle with the cheese and onion. Combine the milk, eggs, salt, and pepper in a bowl. Beat to completely blend. Pour into the prepared pan or shell. With the microwave on LOW, cook for 30 to 35 minutes or until a knife inserted in the middle comes out clean; rotate the dish a quarter turn after 5 minutes, then every 3 minutes—or use a food rotator.

Yield: 8 servings
Exchange, 1 serving (without shell): 1¼ high-fat meat
Calories, 1 serving (without shell): 139
Carbohydrates, 1 serving (without shell): 1

Corned Beef Hash and Eggs

15 oz. can	corned beef hash	429 g can
6	eggs	6

Divide the corned beef hash evenly among six individual microwave dishes. Make an indentation in the hash. Break an egg into each indentation. Prick the yolk with a pin or toothpick. Cover each dish with plastic wrap. With the microwave on MEDIUM, cook for 8 to 9 minutes or until the eggs are almost set; rotate the dishes a quarter turn every 2 minutes or use a food rotator. Allow the eggs and hash to rest for 1 minute before serving.

Yield: 6 servings
Exchange, 1 serving: ½ bread, 1½ medium-fat meat, 1 fat
Calories, 1 serving: 205
Carbohydrates, 1 serving: 8

Cheese and Mushrooms Lunch

1 c.	sliced mushrooms	250 mL
1 T.	reduced-calorie margarine	15 mL
⅔ c.	evaporated skim milk	180 mL
2 c.	shredded processed American cheese	500 mL
6 slices	whole wheat toast	6 slices
	snipped fresh parsley	

Combine the mushrooms and margarine in a 1 qt. (1 L) microwave casserole or baking dish. With the microwave on HIGH, cook for 2 minutes. Stir to rearrange the mushrooms once during cooking. Add the evaporated milk. Return to the microwave and continue cooking on MEDIUM for 1½ minutes or until the milk is warm. Stir in the cheese. Return to the microwave and continue cooking on MEDIUM for 3 to 4 minutes or until the cheese is melted; rotate the dish one-half turn and stir after 2 minutes. Spoon over the toast. Sprinkle with parsley.

Yield: 6 servings
Exchange, 1 serving: 1 bread, 1 whole milk, ⅓ high-fat meat
Calories, 1 serving: 254
Carbohydrates, 1 serving: 17

Sauces

White Sauce

Thin:

1 T.	reduced-calorie margarine	15 mL
1 T.	all-purpose flour	15 mL
1 c.	skim milk	250 mL
	salt to taste	

With the microwave on HIGH, melt the margarine in a 1 qt. (1 L) measuring cup for 30 seconds. Stir in the flour and blend. Slowly add the milk, stirring constantly. Return to the microwave and continue cooking on HIGH for 4 minutes; stir hard after 2 minutes, then every 30 seconds until the mixture is thickened. Add salt to taste.

Yield: 1 cup (250 mL)
Exchange: 1 skim milk, 1 fat, ⅓ bread
Calories: 166
Carbohydrates: 17

For Medium White Sauce: Use 2 T. (30 mL) of reduced-calorie margarine and 2 T. (30 mL) of all-purpose flour.

Yield: 1 cup (250 mL)
Exchange: 1 skim milk, 2 fat, ⅔ bread
Calories: 243
Carbohydrates: 22

For Thick White Sauce: Use 3 T. (45 mL) of reduced-calorie margarine and 3 T. (45 mL) of all-purpose flour.

Yield: 1 cup (250 mL)
Exchange: 1 skim milk, 3 fat, 1 bread
Calories: 320
Carbohydrates: 27

Cheddar Cheese Sauce

2 T.	reduced-calorie margarine	30 mL
2 T.	all-purpose flour	30 mL
1 c.	skim milk	250 mL
¼ t.	salt	1 mL
½ c.	shredded sharp Cheddar cheese	125 mL

With the microwave on HIGH, melt the margarine in a 1 qt. (1 L) measuring cup for 30 seconds. Stir in the flour and blend. Slowly add the milk, stirring constantly. Return to the microwave and continue cooking on HIGH for 4 minutes; stir hard after 2 minutes, then every 30 seconds until the mixture is thickened. Stir in the salt and cheese. Continue cooking on HIGH for 1 minute.

Yield: 4 servings
Exchange, 1 serving: ½ whole milk, ½ high-fat meat
Calories, 1 serving: 122
Carbohydrates, 1 serving: 6

Creole Sauce

¼ c.	green pepper, minced	60 mL
2 T.	chopped onion	30 mL
2 T.	reduced-calorie margarine	30 mL
1½ c.	chopped canned tomatoes	375 mL
¼ c.	sliced mushrooms	60 mL
¼ c.	sliced green olives	60 mL
¼ t.	salt	1 mL
dash	black pepper	dash
1 T.	dry sherry	15 mL

Combine the green pepper, onion, and margarine in a 3 qt. (3 L) microwave casserole or bowl. Cover with a lid or plastic wrap. With the microwave on HIGH, cook for 1 to 1 ½ minutes. Add the tomatoes, mushrooms, and olives. Cover and return to the microwave. Cook on HIGH for 2½ minutes. Stir in the salt, pepper, and sherry.

Yield: 8 servings
Exchange, 1 serving: ⅓ vegetable, ½ fat
Calories, 1 serving: 32
Carbohydrates, 1 serving: 2

Mushroom Sauce

¼ lb.	button mushrooms	125 g
1 T.	reduced-calorie margarine	15 mL
2 T.	all-purpose flour	30 mL
½ c.	water	125 mL
2 t.	instant chicken broth mix	10 mL
½ c.	skim milk	125 mL
	snipped fresh parsley (optional)	

Clean the mushrooms and slice them lengthwise. Combine the sliced mushrooms and margarine in a 2 qt. (2 L) microwave or glass measuring cup. Cover with plastic wrap. With the microwave on HIGH, cook for 2 minutes or until the mushrooms are tender. Blend in the flour. Gradually add the water and chicken broth mix, stirring to completely blend. Cook, uncovered, in the microwave on HIGH for 5 minutes or until the mixture is thickened. Slowly add the miik, stirring constantly. With the microwave on MEDIUM HIGH, cook for 2 minutes, stirring after 1 minute. Continue cooking on MEDIUM to desired thickness. Sprinkle with parsley, if desired.

Yield: 4 servings
Exchange, 1 serving: ½ bread
Calories, 1 serving: 45
Carbohydrates, 1 serving: 7

Gravy

¼ c.	cold water	60 mL
2 T.	all-purpose flour	30 mL
1 t.	instant broth mix (beef or chicken)	5 mL
¾ c.	hot tap water	190 mL

Combine the ¼ c. (60 mL) cold water and flour in a 2 c. (500 mL) microwave measuring cup or bowl or shaker bottle. Stir or shake to blend thoroughly. (If you are using a shaker bottle, transfer to 2 c. (500 mL) bowl.) Dissolve the broth mix in the ¾ c. (190 mL) hot tap water. Gradually stir the hot mixture into the flour mixture. Cook, uncovered, in the microwave on HIGH for 2 minutes, stirring every 30 seconds.

Yield: 4 servings
Exchange, 1 serving: ⅓ bread
Calories, 1 serving: 14
Carbohydrates, 1 serving: 5

Tart Cranberry Sauce

1 c.	raw cranberries	250 mL
¼ c.	water	60 mL
3 T.	granulated fructose	45 mL

Combine all the ingredients in a 1 qt. (1 L) measuring cup. Cover loosely with plastic wrap. With the microwave on HIGH, cook for 4 minutes or until all the cranberries have "popped"; stir after 2 minutes. Remove from the microwave and allow to rest for 2 minutes. Transfer to a serving dish. Serve either hot or chilled.

Yield: 8 servings
Exchange, 1 serving: ⅓ fruit
Calories, 1 serving: 11
Carbohydrates, 1 serving: 4

Hot Tomato Sauce

4	tomatoes	4
4	tabasco peppers	4
1	green bell pepper	1
½	onion	½
1 stalk	celery	1 stalk
⅓ c.	white vinegar	90 mL
2 T.	granulated fructose	30 mL
1 T.	hot pepper sauce	15 mL
½ t.	salt	2 mL
⅛ t.	black pepper	½ mL
dash each	clove and cinnamon	dash each

Clean the vegetables and cut them into chunks. Place the vegetables in a food processor, and process on HIGH for 1 to 1½ minute(s) or until the mixture is finely chopped. Stir and push the vegetables down the sides occasionally. Transfer the vegetables to a 4 qt. (4 L) microwave casserole or bowl. Stir in the remaining ingredients. Cook, uncovered, in the microwave on HIGH for 20 to 30 minutes, depending on the thickness of the sauce desired.

Yield: 20 servings
Exchange, 1 serving: 1 vegetable
Calories, 1 serving: 22
Carbohydrates, 1 serving: 5

Italian Meatless Sauce

2 T.	olive oil	30 mL
2 cloves	garlic, minced	2 cloves
28 oz. can	tomatoes, chopped	800 g can
2 T.	snipped fresh parsley	30 mL
¾ t.	oregano	4 mL
½ t.	salt	2 mL
¼ t.	marjoram	1 mL
⅛ t.	black pepper	½ mL

Combine the oil and garlic in a 2 qt. (2 L) measuring cup. With the microwave on HIGH, cook for 2 minutes. Add the remaining ingredients, stirring to mix. With the microwave on HIGH, cook for 30 seconds to 1 minute.

Yield: 4 servings
Exchange, 1 serving: ½ vegetable, 1 fat
Calories, 1 serving: 65
Carbohydrates, 1 serving: 2

Fresh Applesauce

6	MacIntosh apples	6
½ c.	water	125 mL
¼ c.	granulated sugar replacement	60 mL
	OR	
2 T.	granulated fructose	30 mL

Wash, quarter, and core the apples. Combine the apples and water in a 3 qt. (3 L) microwave casserole or bowl. Cover with a lid or plastic wrap. With the microwave on HIGH, cook for 10 to 12 minutes or until the apples are tender; stir after 5 minutes, then every 2 minutes. Transfer the apples to a food processor (or push through a sieve or food mill). Process on HIGH until the mixture is your desired consistency. Stir in either the sugar replacement or the fructose.

Yield: 8 servings
Exchange, 1 serving (with sugar replacement): 1 fruit
Calories, 1 serving (with sugar replacement): 60
Carbohydrates, 1 serving (with sugar replacement): 15
Exchange, 1 serving (with fructose): 1⅓ fruit
Calories, 1 serving (with fructose): 73
Carbohydrates, 1 serving (with fructose): 17

Quick Barbecue Sauce

1 c.	ketchup	250 mL
¼ c.	white vinegar	60 mL
¼ c.	water	60 mL
1	onion, finely chopped	1
3 T.	granulated brown sugar replacement	45 mL
1½ t.	Worcestershire sauce	7 mL
1 t.	celery seed, crushed	5 mL
¼ t.	salt	1 mL
⅛ t.	garlic powder	½ mL
	black pepper	
	horseradish mustard (optional)	

Combine all the ingredients in a 2 qt. (2 L) measuring cup. Stir to mix. Cover with plastic wrap. With the microwave on HIGH, cook for 2½ to 3 minutes or until the onions are tender.

Yield: 8 servings
Exchange, 1 serving: 1 vegetable
Calories, 1 serving: 30
Carbohydrates, 1 serving: 6

Sweet and Sour Sauce

¼ c.	water	60 mL
2 T.	cider vinegar	30 mL
1 T.	ketchup	15 mL
1 t.	Worcestershire sauce	5 mL
1 c.	unsweetened strawberry jelly	250 mL

Combine the water, cider vinegar, ketchup, and Worcestershire sauce in a 1 qt. (1 L) microwave measuring cup or bowl. Cover with wax paper. With the microwave on HIGH, cook for 1½ to 2 minutes or until the mixture is boiling. Stir in the jelly. Return to the microwave and heat on LOW for 1 to 1½ minutes or just until the jelly is melted. (Do not overheat after the jelly has been added.)

Yield: 1¼ c. (310 mL) or 6 servings
Exchange, 1 serving: negligible
Calories, 1 serving: negligible
Carbohydrates, 1 serving: negligible

Fresh Cucumber Sauce

1 c.	chopped cucumber	250 mL
2 T.	water	30 mL
2 T.	reduced-calorie margarine	30 mL
2 T.	all-purpose flour	30 mL
1 c.	fish broth or water	250 mL
2 t.	lemon juice	10 mL
1 t.	grated lemon rind	5 mL
1 t.	grated onion	5 mL
	salt and pepper to taste	

Combine the cucumber and 2 T. (30 mL) water in a 2 qt. (2 L) microwave measuring cup or bowl. Cover with a lid or plastic wrap. With the microwave on HIGH, cook for 2 to 2½ minutes, stirring after 1 minute. Drain thoroughly and set aside. Melt the margarine in a 1 qt. (1 L) microwave measuring cup or bowl. Completely blend in the flour. Slowly add the 1 c. (250 mL) fish broth or water, stirring constantly. Cook, uncovered, with the microwave on HIGH for 4 to 5 minutes or until the mixture is thickened. Remove from the microwave. Add the lemon juice, rind, onion, salt, and pepper. Stir to completely blend. Now, fold in the cooked cucumber. Allow the mixture to rest 2 to 3 minutes before serving.

Yield: 10 servings
Exchange, 1 serving: ⅓ fat
Calories, 1 serving: 15
Carbohydrates, 1 serving: 1

Hot Lemon Sauce

½ c.	reduced-calorie margarine	125 mL
3 T.	lemon juice	45 mL
1 t.	grated lemon rind	5 mL

Combine all the ingredients in a 2 c. (500 mL) microwave measuring cup or bowl. Cook, uncovered, in the microwave for 2 to 2½ minutes or until the mixture is boiling. Serve hot.

Yield: 8 servings
Exchange, 1 serving: 1 fat
Calories, 1 serving: 47
Carbohydrates, 1 serving: negligible

Desserts

Pastry Shell (from mix)

1   pie crust stick or mix for a 9 in. (23 cm) shell   1

Prepare the dough as directed on the package. Form the dough into a 9 in. (23 cm) microwave or glass pie pan. Trim and flute the edges as desired. Prick the bottom and sides of the unbaked shell. Cook on ME-DIUM HIGH in the microwave for 4 to 5 minutes, rotating the dish one-fourth turn after the first 2 minutes. Allow to cool.

Yield: 8 servings
Exchange, 1 serving: 1 bread, 1 fat
Calories, 1 serving: 123
Carbohydrates, 1 serving: 15

Graham Cracker Crust

⅓ c.   reduced-calorie margarine   90 mL
1½ c.   graham cracker crumbs   375 mL

Melt the margarine in a 9 in. (23 cm) microwave or glass pie dish. Add the graham cracker crumbs. Using a fork, completely blend the crumbs and margarine. Press evenly onto the bottom and sides of the dish. Cook, uncovered, in the microwave on HIGH for 2 minutes; rotate the dish a quarter turn after 1 minute. Allow the crust to rest and cool before filling.

Yield: 8 servings
Exchange, 1 serving: 1 bread, 1 fat
Calories, 1 serving: 120
Carbohydrates, 1 serving: 16

Flaky Pie Crust (two shells)

1½ c.	all-purpose flour	375 mL
¼ t.	salt	1 mL
½ c.	solid vegetable shortening	125 mL
1	egg	1
1 t.	white vinegar	5 mL
2 T.	water	30 mL
2 to 3 drops	yellow food coloring	2 to 3 drops

Sift the flour; then measure and resift into a bowl or food processor. Add the salt and shortening. Using a pastry blender or food processor, cut until the mixture becomes coarse crumbs. In a small bowl, combine the egg, vinegar, water, and food coloring. Lightly beat to blend. Drizzle into the flour mixture, mixing lightly until all the flour is moistened and forms into a ball. Divide the dough in half, roll out each piece on a lightly floured board, and fit into two 9 in. (23 cm) microwave or glass pie dishes. Prick the bottom and sides of each shell. Cook one shell at a time on MEDIUM HIGH in the microwave for 4 to 5 minutes; rotate the dish a quarter turn after 2 minutes, then again in 2 minutes. Allow to cool.

Yield: 16 servings (2 shells)
Exchange, 1 serving: 1 bread, 3 fat
Calories, 1 serving: 214
Carbohydrates, 1 serving: 16

Light Dried-Apricot Topping

1 t.	cornstarch	5 mL
⅔ c.	cold water	180 mL
¼ c.	chopped dried apricots	60 mL

Dissolve the cornstarch in the cold water in a 2 c. (500 mL) microwave bowl. Add the apricots. Cook, uncovered, on HIGH for 1 minute in the microwave. Stir and continue cooking on HIGH for 1½ to 2 minutes or until the mixture is clear. Remove from the microwave, cover with paper towels and allow to cool.

Yield: 3 servings
Exchange, 1 serving: 1 fruit
Calories, 1 serving: 58
Carbohydrates, 1 serving: 14

Strawberry-Pineapple Compote

2 c.	frozen unsweetened strawberries	500 mL
2 cans	pineapple chunks, in their own juice	2 cans
(16 oz. each)		(458 g each)
1 T.	lemon juice	15 mL
2 T.	cornstarch	30 mL

Defrost the strawberries. Place the strawberries and their juice in a 2 qt. (2 L) microwave casserole or bowl. Drain ¼ c. (60 mL) of juice from the pineapple chunks into a measuring cup. Drain off the remaining juice from the pineapple. Add the pineapple chunks to the strawberries in the casserole. Add the lemon juice and cornstarch to the pineapple juice in the measuring cup, stirring to completely blend. Pour the pine-apple-lemon liquid into the strawberry mixture, stirring to completely mix. With the microwave on HIGH, cook for 4 to 6 minutes; rotate the dish a quarter turn after every 60 seconds and stir, or use a food rotator and stir every 60 seconds. Serve either warm or chilled.

Yield: 6 servings
Exchange, 1 serving: 1⅓ fruit
Calories, 1 serving: 81
Carbohydrates, 1 serving: 18

Christmas Cup Pudding

1 T.	all-purpose flour	15 mL
3 pkg. (.10 oz. each)	granulated fructose	3 pkg. (2.8 g each)
1 c.	low-fat milk	250 mL
¼ t.	vanilla extract	1 mL
⅛ t.	butter rum flavoring	½ mL
dash each	cinnamon, nutmeg	dash each

Combine the flour and fructose in a 1 qt. (1 L) microwave measuring cup or bowl. Gradually stir in the milk until the flour is dissolved. Blend in the remaining ingredients. Cook, uncovered, in the micro-wave on HIGH for 3 minutes; rotate the dish a quarter turn and stir thoroughly every 60 seconds.

Yield: 2 servings
Exchange, 1 serving: ½ low-fat milk, ¼ fruit
Calories, 1 serving: 76
Carbohydrates, 1 serving: 3

Apple and Raisin Filling or Pudding

1 qt.	sliced apples	1 L
¾ c.	water	190 mL
1½ T.	all-purpose flour	21 mL
¼ c.	granulated sugar replacement	60 mL
¼ t.	cinnamon	1 mL
1 c.	raisins	250 mL

Combine the apples and water in a 3 qt. (3 L) casserole or bowl. With the microwave on HIGH, cook for 6 minutes. Allow to cool. Stir the flour, sugar replacement and cinnamon into the raisins. Add to the cooled apples. Stir to blend and dissolve the flour. Cover with a lid or plastic wrap. With the microwave on MEDIUM, cook for 10 to 12 minutes or until partially set. Pour into a prepared pie shell or eight individual serving dishes. Allow to cool completely.

Yield: 8 servings
Exchange, 1 serving (without pie shell): 2 fruit
Calories, 1 serving (without pie shell): 123
Carbohydrates, 1 serving (without pie shell): 27

Delightful Rice Pudding

2 c.	skim milk	500 mL
2	eggs, slightly beaten	2
⅓ c.	granulated sugar replacement	90 mL
1½ t.	vanilla extract	7 mL
¼ t.	cinnamon	1 mL
⅛ t.	nutmeg	½ mL
½ c.	quick-cooking rice	125 mL
⅓ c.	raisins	90 mL

Measure the milk in a 1 qt. (1 L) microwave or glass measuring cup. With the microwave on HIGH, cook for 5 minutes or until hot. Combine the remaining ingredients in a 1½ or 2 qt. (1½ or 2 L) microwave casserole or bowl. Stir to mix; then blend in the hot milk. Cover with a lid or plastic wrap. With the microwave on LOW, cook for 12 to 15 minutes or until set. Allow the pudding to rest 5 minutes before serving.

Yield: 6 servings
Exchange, 1 serving: ½ low-fat milk, ½ fruit, ½ bread
Calories, 1 serving: 129
Carbohydrates, 1 serving: 15

Banana Treat

1 c.	evaporated skim milk	250 mL
1 c.	water	250 mL
1	very ripe banana, mashed	1
¼ c.	granulated fructose	60 mL
1 ½ T.	all-purpose flour	21 mL
1 t.	vanilla extract	5 mL
8 T.	prepared nondairy whipped topping	120 mL

Combine the ingredients, except the whipped topping, in a 2 qt. (2 L) microwave bowl or measuring cup. Stir to blend. Cook, uncovered, in the microwave on HIGH for 5 minutes. Stir to thoroughly blend. Continue cooking on MEDIUM for 3 minutes, reduce heat to LOW, and cook for 4 more minutes. Stir occasionally during cooking. Top each serving with 1 T. (15 mL) of whipped topping.

Yield: 8 servings
Exchange, 1 serving (with topping): ½ fruit, ⅓ skim milk
Calories, 1 serving (with topping): 61
Carbohydrates, 1 serving (with topping): 12

Baked Custard

1¾ c.	skim milk	440 mL
¼ c.	granulated sugar replacement	60 mL
3	eggs	3
1 t.	vanilla extract	5 mL
dash	salt	dash
	nutmeg (optional)	

Combine the ingredients, except the nutmeg, in a 1 qt. (1 L) bowl or measuring cup. Beat with a fork to blend thoroughly. Pour into six individual microwave or glass custard cups. If desired, sprinkle with nutmeg. Cook, uncovered, in the microwave on MEDIUM LOW for 15 minutes or until a knife inserted in the middle comes out almost clean; rearrange the custard cups about every 5 minutes for uniform cooking or use a food rotator. Allow the custard to rest 5 minutes before serving.

Yield: 6 servings
Exchange, 1 serving: ½ medium-fat meat, ¼ skim milk
Calories, 1 serving: 60
Carbohydrates, 1 serving: 3

Recipes from Nabisco

These recipes are from the Nabisco cookbooks, *Diet for a Healthy Heart*, *Sodium Sense*, and *Eating to Your Heart's Content*. For further information write:

Nabisco Brands Inc.
P.O. 1937
East Hanover, New Jersey 07936-1937

Chinese-Style Fish and Snow Peas

Yield: 4 servings

3 T.	Fleischmann's Sweet Unsalted Margarine
½ c.	chopped scallions
1 clove	garlic, minced
1 lb.	cod fillets, cut into 1 in. squares
¼ c.	low-sodium chicken broth
3 T.	cider vinegar
1 t.	dry mustard
½ t.	ground ginger
1 pkg.	(6 oz.) snow peas, thawed
2 c.	hot cooked rice, prepared without added salt

In a 2-qt. microwave-proof casserole, place the margarine, scallions, and garlic. Microwave on HIGH for 3 minutes, stirring after 2 minutes. Add the fish, broth, vinegar, mustard, and ginger; cover. Microwave on HIGH for 5 minutes, stirring after 3 minutes. Add the snow peas. Microwave on HIGH for 1 to 2 minutes. Serve over rice.

Nutritional Information per serving:
Calories: 311
Sodium (mg): 88
Cholesterol (mg): 57
Fat (mg): 9
Exchange values: 3 meats I
                 2 grains I

Bran-Raisin Muffins

Yield: 1 dozen

1¼ c.	Nabisco 100% Bran
¾ c.	skim milk
½ c.	orange juice
¼ c.	Egg Beaters
¼ c.	Fleischmann's Sweet Unsalted Margarine, melted
1¼ c.	all-purpose flour
¼ c.	sugar
2½ t.	baking powder
½ t.	baking soda
½ c.	dark seedless raisins

In a medium bowl, combine Nabisco 100% Bran, the skim milk, and orange juice; let stand 5 minutes. Stir in the Egg Beaters and Fleischmann's Sweet Unsalted Margarine until blended. In small bowl, combine the flour, sugar, baking powder, and baking soda; stir into the bran mixture just until moistened. Stir in the raisins. Spoon half the batter into six greased 6 oz. custard cups. Arrange the cups in a circle in the microwave. Microwave on HIGH for 3 to 4 minutes, rearranging the cups after 1½ minutes. Repeat with the remaining batter. Serve warm.

Nutritional Information per serving:
Calories: 148
Sodium (mg): 191
Cholesterol (mg): 0
Fat (mg): 4
Exchange Values: 1½ grains II
                ½ fat

Spinach Balls

Yield: 3 dozen appetizers

1 pkg.	(10 oz.) frozen chopped spinach, thawed and well drained
1 c.	herbed stuffing mix
1 sm.	onion, chopped
¾ c.	Egg Beaters
	OR
	Egg Beaters with Cheez
1 T.	Fleischmann's margarine, melted

In a medium bowl, combine the spinach, stuffing mix, and onion.

Blend in the Egg Beaters and Fleischmann's margarine. Shape into 1-in. balls. Arrange 12 balls in a 9 in. microwave-proof pie plate. Microwave on HIGH for 2½ to 3 minutes, rotating the dish one-half turn after 1½ minutes. Repeat with the remaining spinach balls. Serve warm.

To Freeze: Prepare as above; cool. Wrap and freeze. To reheat, arrange the frozen appetizers on a baking sheet. Bake at 350° F for 10 to 15 minutes or until hot.

Nutritional Information per serving:

	Egg Beaters	Egg Beaters with Cheez
Calories:	16	18
Sodium (mg):	43	50
Cholesterol (mg):	0	0
Fat (mg):	1	1
Exchange Values:	½ vegetable	½ vegetable
	⅛ fat	⅛ fat

Italian Vegetable Stir-Fry

Yield: 6 servings

¼ c.	Fleischmann's Sweet Unsalted Margarine
1 clove	garlic, crushed
1 med.	eggplant, cubed (about 1 lb.)
2 sm.	zucchini, sliced
1½ c.	sliced mushrooms
2	red peppers, sliced
1 sm.	onion, sliced
2 T.	chopped parsley
1½ t.	basil leaves
⅛ t.	ground black pepper

In a 4-qt. microwave-proof casserole, place the margarine and garlic; cover. Microwave on HIGH for 2½ to 3 minutes. Add the remaining ingredients; cover. Microwave on HIGH for 9 to 10 minutes, stirring after 5 minutes. Let stand, covered, 5 minutes before serving.

Nutritional Information per serving:
Calories: 143
Sodium (mg): 28
Cholesterol (mg): 0
Fat (mg): 8
Exchange values: 3 vegetables
1½ fats I

Turkey Meatballs with Honey Mustard Sauce

Yield: 28 appetizers

1 lb.	ground raw turkey
⅓ c.	Nabisco cracker meal
¼ c.	Egg Beaters
	or
	Egg Beaters with Cheez
¼ c.	chopped onion
2¼ t.	dry mustard
½ t.	tarragon leaves
1 c.	unsweetened pineapple juice
1 T.	cornstarch
1 T.	dry sherry, optional

In a medium bowl, thoroughly mix the turkey, Nabisco cracker meal, Egg Beaters, onion, ¼ teaspoon dry mustard, and tarragon. Shape into 28 (1¼ in.) balls. Arrange 14 meatballs in a 9 in. microwave-proof pie plate. Microwave on HIGH (100 percent power) for 5 minutes, turning after 3 minutes. Repeat with the remaining meatballs. To make the sauce, combine the remaining ingredients in 2-cup microwave-proof measuring cup. Microwave on HIGH for 3 minutes, stirring after 1½ minutes. Serve as a dipping sauce with the meatballs.

To Freeze: Prepare as above; cool. Wrap and freeze. To reheat, arrange the appetizers on a baking sheet. Bake at 350 °F for 10 to 15 minutes.

Nutritional information per serving:

	Egg Beaters	Egg Beaters with Cheez
Calories	44	45
Sodium(mg)	20	24
Cholesterol(mg)	11	11
Fat(mg)	2	2
Exchange values:	½ meat	½ meat
	¼ grain I	¼ grain I

EXCHANGE LISTS

The reason for dividing food into six different groups is that foods vary in their carbohydrate, protein, fat, and calorie content. Each exchange list contains foods that are alike—each choice contains about the same amount of carbohydrate, protein, fat, and calories.

The following chart shows the amount of these nutrients in one serving from each exchange list.

Exchange List	Carbohydrate (grams)	Protein (grams)	Fat (grams)	Calories
Starch/Bread	15	3	trace	80
Meat				
Lean	—	7	3	55
Medium-Fat	—	7	5	75
High-Fat	—	7	8	100
Vegetable	5	2	—	25
Fruit	15	—	—	60
Milk				
Skim	12	8	trace	90
Lowfat	12	8	5	120
Whole	12	8	8	150
Fat	—	—	5	45

As you read the exchange lists, you will notice that one choice often is a larger amount of food than another choice from the same list. Because foods are so different, each food is measured or weighed so the amount of carbohydrate, protein, fat, and calories is the same in each choice.

You will notice symbols on some foods in the exchange groups. Foods that are high in fiber (3 grams or more per exchange) have this ✍ symbol. High-fiber foods are good for you. It is important to eat more of these foods.

Foods that are high in sodium (400 milligrams or more of sodium per exchange) have this 🍃 symbol; foods that have 400 mg or more of sodium if two or more exchanges are eaten have this ★ symbol. It's a good idea to limit your intake of high-salt foods, especially if you have high blood pressure.

If you have a favorite food that is not included in any of these groups, ask your dietitian about it. That food can probably be worked into your meal plan, at least now and then.

The exchange lists are the basis of a meal planning system designed by a committee of the American Diabetes Association and the American Dietetic Association. While designed primarily for people with diabetes and others who must follow special diets, the exchange lists are based on principles of good nutrition that apply to everyone. ©1989 American Diabetes Association, American Dietetic Association.

1

STARCH / BREAD LIST

E ach item in this list contains approximately 15 grams of carbohydrate, 3 grams of protein, a trace of fat, and 80 calories. Whole grain products average about 2 grams of fiber per exchange. Some foods are higher in fiber. Those foods that contain 3 or more grams of fiber per exchange are identified with the fiber symbol 🌾.

You can choose your starch exchanges from any of the items on this list. If you want to eat a starch food that is not on this list, the general rule is that:

- 1/2 cup of cereal, grain or pasta is one exchange
- 1 ounce of a bread product is one exchange

Your dietitian can help you be more exact.

CEREALS/GRAINS/PASTA

🌾 Bran cereals, concentrated (such as Bran Buds® All Bran®)	1/3 cup
🌾 Bran cereals, flaked	1/2 cup
Bulgur (cooked)	1/2 cup
Cooked cereals	1/2 cup
Cornmeal (dry)	2 1/2 Tbsp.
Grape-Nuts®	3 Tbsp.
Grits (cooked)	1/2 cup
Other ready-to-eat unsweetened cereals	3/4 cup
Pasta (cooked)	1/2 cup
Puffed cereal	1 1/2 cup
Rice, white or brown (cooked)	1/3 cup
Shredded wheat	1/2 cup
🌾 Wheat germ	3 Tbsp.

DRIED BEANS/PEAS/LENTILS

🌾 Beans and peas (cooked) (such as kidney, white, split, blackeye)	1/3 cup
🌾 Lentils (cooked)	1/3 cup
🌾 Baked beans	1/4 cup

STARCHY VEGETABLES

🌾 Corn	1/2 cup
🌾 Corn on cob, 6 in. long	1
🌾 Lima beans	1/2 cup

🌾 Peas, green (canned or frozen)	1/2 cup
🌾 Plantain	1/2 cup
Potato, baked	1 small (3 oz.)
Potato, mashed	1/2 cup
🌾 Squash, winter (acorn, butternut)	1 cup
Yam, sweet potato, plain	1/3 cup

BREAD

Bagel	1/2 (1 oz.)
Bread sticks, crisp, 4 in. long × 1/2 in.	2 (2/3 oz.)
Croutons, lowfat	1 cup
English muffin	1/2
Frankfurter or hamburger bun	1/2 (1 oz.)
Pita, 6 in. across	1/2
Plain roll, small	1 (1 oz.)
Raisin, unfrosted	1 slice (1 oz.)
Rye, pumpernickel	1 slice (1 oz.)
Tortilla, 6 in. across	1
White (including French, Italian)	1 slice (1 oz.)
Whole wheat	1 slice (1 oz.)

🌾 *3 grams or more of fiber per exchange*

CRACKERS/SNACKS

Animal crackers	8
Graham crackers, 2 1/2 in. square	3
Matzoh	3/4 oz.
Melba toast	5 slices
Oyster crackers	24
Popcorn (popped, no fat added)	3 cups
Pretzels	3/4 oz.
✒ Rye crisp, 2 in. × 3 1/2 in.	4
Saltine-type crackers	6
✒ Whole-wheat crackers, no fat added (crisp breads, such as Finn®, Kavli®, Wasa®)	2-4 slices (3/4 oz.)
Taco shell, 6 in. across	2
Waffle, 4 1/2 in. square	1
✒ Whole-wheat crackers, fat added (such as Triscuit®)	4-6 (1 oz.)

STARCH FOODS PREPARED WITH FAT

(Count as 1 starch/bread exchange, plus 1 fat exchange.)

Biscuit, 2 1/2 in. across	1
Chow mein noodles	1/2 cup
Corn bread, 2 in. cube	1 (2 oz.)
Cracker, round butter type	6
French fried potatoes, 2 in. to 3 1/2 in. long	10 (1 1/2 oz.)
Muffin, plain, small	1
Pancake, 4 in. across	2
Stuffing, bread (prepared)	1/4 cup

MEAT LIST

ach serving of meat and substitutes on this list contains about 7 grams of protein. The amount of fat and number of calories varies, depending on what kind of meat or substitute you choose. The list is divided into three parts based on the amount of fat and calories: lean meat, medium-fat meat, and high-fat meat. One ounce (one meat exchange) of each of these includes:

	Carbohydrate (grams)	Protein (grams)	Fat (grams)	Calories
Lean	0	7	3	55
Medium-Fat	0	7	5	75
High-Fat	0	7	8	100

You are encouraged to use more lean and medium-fat meat, poultry, and fish in your meal plan. This will help decrease your fat intake, which may help decrease your risk for heart disease. The items from the high-fat group are high in saturated fat, cholesterol, and calories. You should limit your choices from the high-fat group to three (3) times per week. Meat and substitutes do not contribute any fiber to your meal plan.

Meats and meat substitutes that have 400 milligrams or more of sodium per exchange are indicated with this symbol.

Meats and meat substitutes that have 400 mg or more of sodium if two or more exchanges are eaten are indicated with this symbol.

TIPS

1. Bake, roast, broil, grill, or boil these foods rather than frying them with added fat.

2. Use a nonstick pan spray or a nonstick pan to brown or fry these foods.

3. Trim off visible fat before and after cooking.

4. Do not add flour, bread crumbs, coating mixes, or fat to these foods when preparing them.

5. Weigh meat after removing bones and fat, and after cooking. Three ounces of cooked meat is about equal to 4 ounces of raw meat. Some examples of meat portions are:

   2 ounces meat (2 meat exchanges) =
     1 small chicken leg or thigh
     1/2 cup cottage cheese or tuna

   3 ounces meat (3 meat exchanges) =
     1 medium pork chop
     1 small hamburger
     1/2 of a whole chicken breast
     1 unbreaded fish fillet
     cooked meat, about the size of a
       deck of cards

6. Restaurants usually serve prime cuts of meat, which are high in fat and calories.

LEAN MEAT AND SUBSTITUTES
(One exchange is equal to any one of the following items.)

Beef: USDA Select or Choice grades of lean beef, such as round, sirloin, and flank steak; tenderloin; and chipped beef 🖛 — 1 oz.

Pork: Lean pork, such as fresh ham; canned, cured or boiled ham 🖛 , Canadian bacon 🖛 , tenderloin. — 1 oz.

Veal: All cuts are lean except for veal cutlets (ground or cubed). Examples of lean veal are chops and roasts. — 1 oz.

Poultry: Chicken, turkey, Cornish hen (without skin) — 1 oz.

Fish:
All fresh and frozen fish	1 oz.
Crab, lobster, scallops, shrimp, clams (fresh or canned in water)	2 oz.
Oysters	6 medium
Tuna ★ (canned in water)	1/4 cup
Herring ★ (uncreamed or smoked)	1 oz.
Sardines (canned)	2 medium

Wild Game:
Venison, rabbit, squirrel	1 oz.
Pheasant, duck, goose (without skin)	1 oz.

Cheese:
Any cottage cheese ★	1/4 cup
Grated parmesan	2 Tbsp.
Diet cheeses 🖛 (with less than 55 calories per ounce)	1 oz.

Other:
95% fat-free luncheon meat 🖛	1 1/2 oz.
Egg whites	3 whites
Egg substitutes with less than 55 calories per 1/2 cup	1/2 cup

---

🖛 *400 mg or more of sodium per exchange*

★ *400 mg or more of sodium if two or more exchanges are eaten*

MEDIUM-FAT MEAT AND SUBSTITUTES
(One exchange is equal to any one of the following items.)

Beef: Most beef products fall into this category. Examples are: all ground beef, roast (rib, chuck, rump), steak (cubed, Porterhouse, T-bone), and meatloaf. — 1 oz.

Pork: Most pork products fall into this category. Examples are: chops, loin roast, Boston butt, cutlets. — 1 oz.

Lamb: Most lamb products fall into this category. Examples are: chops, leg, and roast. — 1 oz.

Veal: Cutlet (ground or cubed, unbreaded) — 1 oz.

Poultry: Chicken (with skin), domestic duck or goose (well drained of fat), ground turkey — 1 oz.

Fish:
Tuna ★ (canned in oil and drained)	1/4 cup
Salmon ★ (canned)	1/4 cup

Cheese: Skim or part-skim milk cheeses, such as:
Ricotta	1/4 cup
Mozzarella	1 oz.
Diet cheeses 🖛 (with 56-80 calories per ounce)	1 oz.

Other:
86% fat-free luncheon meat ★	1 oz.
Egg (high in cholesterol, limit to 3 per week)	1
Egg substitutes with 56-80 calories per 1/4 cup	1/4 cup
Tofu (2 1/2 in. × 2 3/4 in. × 1 in.)	4 oz.
Liver, heart, kidney, sweetbreads (high in cholesterol)	1 oz.

🖛 *400 mg or more of sodium per exchange*

400 mg or more of sodium if two or more exchanges are eaten

HIGH-FAT MEAT AND SUBSTITUTES

Remember, these items are high in saturated fat, cholesterol, and calories, and should be used only three (3) times per week.

(One exchange is equal to any one of the following items.)

Beef:	Most USDA Prime cuts of beef, such as ribs, corned beef	1 oz.
Pork:	Spareribs, ground pork, pork sausage 🐟 (patty or link)	1 oz.
Lamb:	Patties (ground lamb)	1 oz.
Fish:	Any fried fish product	1 oz.
Cheese:	All regular cheeses, such as American 🐟, Blue 🐟, Cheddar , Monterey Jack , Swiss	1 oz.
Other:	Luncheon meat 🐟 , such as bologna, salami, pimento loaf	1 oz.
	Sausage 🐟 , such as Polish, Italian smoked	1 oz.
	Knockwurst 🐟	1 oz.
	Bratwurst	1 oz.
	Frankfurter 🐟 (turkey or chicken)	1 frank (10/lb.)
	Peanut butter (contains unsaturated fat)	1 Tbsp.

Count as one high-fat meat plus one fat exchange:

Frankfurter 🐟 (beef, pork, or combination)	1 frank (10/lb.)

🐟 *400 mg or more of sodium per exchange*

400 mg or more of sodium if two or more exchanges are eaten

3
VEGETABLE LIST

Each vegetable serving on this list contains about 5 grams of carbohydrate, 2 grams of protein, and 25 calories.

Vegetables contain 2-3 grams of dietary fiber. Vegetables which contain 400 mg or more of sodium per exchange are identified with a 🌾 symbol.

Vegetables are a good source of vitamins and minerals. Fresh and frozen vegetables have more vitamins and less added salt. Rinsing canned vegetables will remove much of the salt.

Unless otherwise noted, the serving size for vegetables (one vegetable exchange) is:

1/2 cup of cooked vegetables or vegetable juice

1 cup of raw vegetables

Artichoke (1/2 medium)
Asparagus
Beans (green, wax, Italian)
Bean sprouts
Beets
Broccoli
Brussels sprouts
Cabbage, cooked
Carrots
Cauliflower
Eggplant
Greens (collard, mustard, turnip)
Kohlrabi
Leeks

Mushrooms, cooked
Okra
Onions
Pea pods
Peppers (green)
Rutabaga
Sauerkraut 🌾
Spinach, cooked
Summer squash (crookneck)
Tomato (one large)
Tomato/vegetable juice 🌾
Turnips
Water chestnuts
Zucchini, cooked

Starchy vegetables such as corn, peas, and potatoes are found on the Starch/Bread List.

🌾 *400 mg or more of sodium per exchange*

4
FRUIT LIST

Each item on this list contains about 15 grams of
carbohydrate and 60 calories. Fresh, frozen, and dried fruits
have about 2 grams of fiber per exchange. Fruits that have 3
or more grams of fiber per exchange have a ✍
symbol. Fruit juices contain very little dietary fiber.

The carbohydrate and calorie content for a fruit exchange
are based on the usual serving of the most commonly eaten
fruits. Use fresh fruits or fruits frozen or canned without sugar
added. Whole fruit is more filling than fruit juice and may be a
better choice for those who are trying to lose weight. Unless
otherwise noted, the serving size for one fruit exchange is:

> 1/2 cup of fresh fruit or fruit juice
> 1/4 cup of dried fruit

FRESH, FROZEN, AND UNSWEETENED CANNED FRUIT

Apple (raw, 2 in. across)	1 apple
Applesauce (unsweetened)	1/2 cup
Apricots (medium, raw)	4 apricots
Apricots (canned)	1/2 cup, or 4 halves
Banana (9 in. long)	1/2 banana
✍ Blackberries (raw)	3/4 cup
✍ Blueberries (raw)	3/4 cup
Cantaloupe (5 in. across) (cubes)	1/3 melon 1 cup
Cherries (large, raw)	12 cherries
Cherries (canned)	1/2 cup
Figs (raw, 2 in. across)	2 figs
Fruit cocktail (canned)	1/2 cup
Grapefruit (medium)	1/2 grapefruit
Grapefruit (segments)	3/4 cup
Grapes (small)	15 grapes
Honeydew melon (medium) (cubes)	1/8 melon 1 cup
Kiwi (large)	1 kiwi
Mandarin oranges	3/4 cup
Mango (small)	1/2 mango
✍ Nectarine (2 1/2 in. across)	1 nectarine
Orange (2 1/2 in. across)	1 orange
Papaya	1 cup
Peach (2 3/4 in. across)	1 peach, or 3/4 cup
Peaches (canned)	1/2 cup or 2 halves
Pear	1/2 large, or 1 small

Pears (canned)	1/2 cup, or 2 halves
Persimmon (medium, native)	2 persimmons
Pineapple (raw)	3/4 cup
Pineapple (canned)	1/3 cup
Plum (raw, 2 in. across)	2 plums
✍ Pomegranate	1/2 pomegranate
✍ Raspberries (raw)	1 cup
✍ Strawberries (raw, whole)	1 1/4 cup
✍ Tangerine (2 1/2 in. across)	2 tangerines
Watermelon (cubes)	1 1/4 cup

DRIED FRUIT

✍ Apples	4 rings
✍ Apricots	7 halves
Dates	2 1/2 medium
✍ Figs	1 1/2
✍ Prunes	3 medium
Raisins	2 Tbsp.

FRUIT JUICE

Apple juice/cider	1/2 cup
Cranberry juice cocktail	1/3 cup
Grapefruit juice	1/2 cup
Grape juice	1/3 cup
Orange juice	1/2 cup
Pineapple juice	1/2 cup
Prune juice	1/3 cup

✍ 3 or more grams of fiber per exchange

5
MILK LIST

ach serving of milk or milk products on this list contains about 12 grams of carbohydrate and 8 grams of protein. The amount of fat in milk is measured in percent (%) of butterfat. The calories vary, depending on what kind of milk you choose. The list is divided into three parts based on the amount of fat and calories: skim/very lowfat milk, lowfat milk, and whole milk. One serving (one milk exchange) of each of these includes:

	Carbohydrate (grams)	Protein (grams)	Fat (grams)	Calories
Skim/Very Lowfat	12	8	trace	90
Lowfat	12	8	5	120
Whole	12	8	8	150

Milk is the body's main source of calcium, the mineral needed for growth and repair of bones. Yogurt is also a good source of calcium. Yogurt and many dry or powdered milk products have different amounts of fat. If you have questions about a particular item, read the label to find out the fat and calorie content.

Milk is good to drink, but it can also be added to cereal, and to other foods. Many tasty dishes such as sugar-free pudding are made with milk. Add life to plain yogurt by adding one of your fruit exchanges to it.

SKIM AND VERY LOWFAT MILK

skim milk	1 cup
1/2% milk	1 cup
1% milk	1 cup
lowfat buttermilk	1 cup
evaporated skim milk	1/2 cup
dry nonfat milk	1/3 cup
plain nonfat yogurt	8 oz.

LOWFAT MILK

2% milk	1 cup fluid
plain lowfat yogurt (with added nonfat milk solids)	8 oz.

WHOLE MILK

The whole milk group has much more fat per serving than the skim and lowfat groups. Whole milk has more than 3 1/4% butterfat. Try to limit your choices from the whole milk group as much as possible.

whole milk	1 cup
evaporated whole milk	1/2 cup
whole plain yogurt	8 oz.

6
FAT LIST

Each serving on the fat list contains about 5 grams of fat and 45 calories.

The foods on the fat list contain mostly fat, although some items may also contain a small amount of protein. All fats are high in calories and should be carefully measured. Everyone should modify fat intake by eating unsaturated fats instead of saturated fats. The sodium content of these foods varies widely. Check the label for sodium information.

UNSATURATED FATS

Avocado	1/8 medium
Margarine	1 tsp.
★ Margarine, diet	1 Tbsp.
Mayonnaise	1 tsp.
★ Mayonnaise, reduced-calorie	1 Tbsp.
Nuts and Seeds:	
Almonds, dry roasted	6 whole
Cashews, dry roasted	1 Tbsp.
Pecans	2 whole
Peanuts	20 small or 10 large
Walnuts	2 whole
Other nuts	1 Tbsp.
Seeds, pine nuts, sun-flower (without shells)	1 Tbsp.
Pumpkin seeds	2 tsp.
Oil (corn, cottonseed, safflower, soybean, sunflower, olive, peanut)	1 tsp.
Olives	10 small or 5 large
Salad dressing, mayonnaise-type	2 tsp.
Salad dressing, mayonnaise-type, reduced-calorie	1 Tbsp.
Salad dressing (oil varieties)	1 Tbsp.

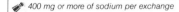 Salad dressing, reduced-calorie   2 Tbsp.

(Two tablespoons of low-calorie salad dressing is a free food.)

SATURATED FATS

Butter	1 tsp.
★ Bacon	1 slice
Chitterlings	1/2 ounce
Coconut, shredded	2 Tbsp.
Coffee whitener, liquid	2 Tbsp.
Coffee whitener, powder	4 tsp.
Cream (light, coffee, table)	2 Tbsp.
Cream, sour	2 Tbsp.
Cream (heavy, whipping)	1 Tbsp.
Cream cheese	1 Tbsp.
★ Salt pork	1/4 ounce

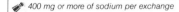 *400 mg or more of sodium per exchange*

★   *400 mg or more of sodium if two or more exchanges are eaten*

Index